William Alexander

The Leading Ideas of the Gospels

five sermons preached before the University of Oxford in 1870-81871

William Alexander

The Leading Ideas of the Gospels

five sermons preached before the University of Oxford in 1870-81871

ISBN/EAN: 9783337088033

Printed in Europe, USA, Canada, Australia, Japan

Cover: Foto ©Lupo / pixelio.de

More available books at **www.hansebooks.com**

THE LEADING IDEAS

OF

THE GOSPELS.

THE LEADING IDEAS

OF

THE GOSPELS.

FIVE SERMONS

PREACHED

BEFORE THE UNIVERSITY OF OXFORD

IN

1870–1871.

BY

WILLIAM ALEXANDER, D.D.

Brasenose College;
Lord Bishop of Derry and Raphoe;
Select Preacher.

London

MACMILLAN AND CO.

1872.

TO THE

REV. FRANCIS KNYVETT LEIGHTON, D.D.

WARDEN OF ALL SOULS',

LATE VICE-CHANCELLOR OF OXFORD,

BY WHOSE APPOINTMENT

THEY WERE PREACHED,

THESE SERMONS ARE DEDICATED

WITH SINCERE RESPECT AND

ESTEEM BY

WILLIAM DERRY AND RAPHOE.

PALACE, DERRY,
January 17, 1872.

CONTENTS.

SERMON I.

ST. MATTHEW.

St. Matt. i. 1.

The Book of the generation of Jesus Christ, the Son of David, the Son of Abraham 1

SERMON II.

ST. MARK.

St. Mark i. 1.

The beginning of the Gospel of Jesus Christ, the Son of God . . . 36

SERMON III.

ST. LUKE.

St. Luke i. 3.

It seemed good to me also, having had perfect understanding of all things from the very first, to write unto thee in order, most excellent Theophilus . 79

SERMON IV.

ST. JOHN.

St. John i. 1, 14.

The Word was God. And the Word was made flesh — 115

SERMON V.

ST. JOHN.

St. John i. 1, 14.

The Word was God. And the Word was made flesh . 152

SERMON I.

ST. MATTHEW.

St. Matthew i. 1.

The Book of the generation of Jesus Christ, the Son of David, the Son of Abraham.

To consider the Four Gospels as regular biographies of our Lord is an error which has logically led to serious consequences. The Gospel is, in the strictest sense, one εὐαγγέλιον τετράμορφον. But the four Evangelists represent that great Life, as four painters might represent a vast range of mountains from four different points of view. Each, having his materials fully before him, arranges and moulds them according to certain leading thoughts, certain fundamental conceptions.

On this Sunday, and next Sunday, and on a few subsequent occasions, I hope to bring before you the fundamental conceptions, the leading ideas of the Four Gospels. Abundant materials for the execution of such a task are of course to be found in the ample stores of theological criticism, ancient and modern. Those whose duty it has been to bring the results of these enormous materials before an audience like the present have generally proposed to themselves a more difficult aim than that which I contemplate. I simply take the books as they are, and ask by what presiding purpose each of them is directed.

I. The Gospel of St. Matthew is pervaded by two leading thoughts, and follows two fundamental conceptions.

1. It is the Gospel of the Discourses. St. Matthew indeed is, in a good sense, σωματικός as opposed to πνευματικός. He does not record such discourses as that concerning the Bread of Life, nor such words as those which were breathed forth among the inner circle in the Guest-chamber. Still, as Renan says, 'a glory which

is at once gentle and terrible, a divine power underlines the words of Jesus in St. Matthew.' Many chapters are filled with the record of His teaching.—I need only indicate the Sermon on the Mount; the instruction to the Apostles upon their first Mission[1]; the cluster of the Parables of the Kingdom[2]; the eightfold woe in the twenty-third Chapter; the eschatological predictions and Parables in the twenty-fourth and twenty-fifth Chapters.

A brief answer may suffice to certain questions which have been asked, apparently for the purpose of disturbing simple Christians in the quiet enjoyment of their Master's words. How do you know that it is, indeed, the very echo of His voice which comes to you across the gulf of time? Was there a reporter in the Apostolic company, who could write short-hand, and take sufficient notes? Are not these Discourses like the speeches in Thucydides or Livy? As Christians, we are satisfied with that sentence, 'The Comforter, which is the Holy Ghost, shall teach

---

[1] St. Matthew x. [2] Ibid. xiii.

you all things'—that is, all things not of the first Creation, which is the object of science, but of the second, which is the object of Revelation:—' and bring all things to your remembrance, whatsoever I have said unto you.' There is no tablet like a loving memory, no Remembrancer like God the Holy Ghost.

2. I pass on to the second great leading idea of St. Matthew's Gospel.

We will not enquire whether the ancient tradition, that this Gospel was originally written in Hebrew (affirmed by Papias, Irenæus, Clement of Alexandria, Tertullian and others, but since the time of Erasmus warmly contested), is true or false. But at all events, with its contents before us, we need not hesitate to say that it bears the same relation to the other Gospels which the Epistle to the Hebrews bears to the other Epistles. It is the Gospel of Types in history, in law, in worship, accomplishing themselves, unrecognised by those to whom they specially pertained. It is the Gospel of Prophecy, accumulating and interweaving its marvellous coincidences (sometimes in dark sayings like those of the thirty pieces of silver, and of the going before the disciples into Galilee [1]) round the Birth and Life, the Death and Resurrection, of Jesus. It is the Gospel of the Christ, crowning the aspirations of saints and seers, but not the carnal expectations of the Jews. It is the Gospel of true Judaism, as opposed to the corrupt Judaism of Priests and Scribes, of Pharisees and Sadducees.

This is written on its forefront. 'The Book of the Generation [2],' not 'the History of the Childhood,' but the ' Liber de Originibus Jesu '— Jesus the Messiah; the Child of Abraham, in Whom all families are to be blessed; the Royal Heir of David's throne, yet rejected by the Jews.

(*a*) In the few opening chapters Prophecy marks Him for its own. 'That it might be fulfilled' is the often recurring formula. He is the Virgin's Son promised to Israel. His Name Jesus, God

---

[1] St. Matthew xxvii. 9, Zechariah xi. 12, 13; St. Matthew xxvi. 31, 32, Zechariah xiii. 7.

[2] βίβλος γενέσεως, St. Matthew i. 1.

the Saviour, is practically the equivalent of Emmanuel. From the mines and forests of the dim mysterious East, gold and incense are brought to the Babe born in Bethlehem. Like the collective Israel, the Personal Israel, God's Servant, is called out of Egypt, to accomplish the redemption which the historical Israel had failed to effect[1]. Round the awful cradle of the new-born King the sobs of Rachel rise, in a grief whose anguish echoes Jeremiah's strain of sorrow. He grows up in Nazareth, that the prediction of all the prophets[2] might be fulfilled, who said, 'He shall be an enigma, despised of men, yet adored by those who despise Him; for he who calls Jesus Nazarene shall against his will call Him, "My Saviour, My Protector[3]."' The voice of the Forerunner, announced by Isaiah and Malachi, prepares His way. He dwells in Capernaum, that the light seen by Isaiah, a richer dawn than ever flushed the Syrian sky, may shine down upon the people that sit in darkness and the

---

[1] St. Matthew ii. 15, Hosea xi. 1. [2] διὰ τῶν προφητῶν, St. Matthew ii. 23. [3] See Appendix, Note 1.

shadow of death [1]. Yet all the sign which Israel gives is this,—that when the Wise Men come from the East to Jerusalem, they are near being murdered by the false king of the Jews. And the Chief Priests and Scribes of the people never visit the place to which, with prophecy in their hands, they had guided others.

The same view pervades every portion of the book. In the Sermon on the Mount, One speaks to us Who is a new and a greater Moses—Who has come by the one great stroke of His life and death to fill up [2] the faint sketch of the Law —to give a new law to men endowed with a new spirit.

Again, in the eighth and ninth Chapters we have that ascending series of miracles, beginning with the victory over disease close at hand or far off, passing on through the calmed waters and the dispossessed demoniacs, until it finds its culminating point in forgiven sin and vanquished death. What is the first special miracle recorded

---

[1] St. Matthew iii. 12 sqq.; Isaiah ix. 1, 2.
[2] πληρῶσαι, v. 17. See Appendix, Note 2.

by St. Matthew?—The healing of the leper. Why does it stand first? Morally and spiritually, no doubt, it follows the Sermon on the Mount, to tell how the eternal leprosy that cleaves to our race can alone be healed. Not merely by words. Not by systems of morality whether they call themselves dependent, independent, or of the Will of God. Not by speaking royally, like a distant king from a cloud of purple and gold; nor roughly, like the policeman who bids misery clear the way; nor patronisingly, like the hard kind of good people, who have never been tempted in some directions themselves, and drop down loving texts into the sinner's sore, with such acidulated accents of severe virtue, that the wound smarts and throbs; nor sentimentally, like popular preachers and the 'feeble folk' who write stories for little children which harden the hearts they are intended to touch. But by coming down from the mountain, and entering into fellowship with the leper; by putting out the hand, and touching the poor defiled thing, and then, in Christ's spirit, saying to it, 'Be thou clean.' But it is also significant that the very miracle stands in the front of St. Matthew's Gospel, which would above all others impress a reader who knew the ritual law with the conviction that the Healer of leprosy was the Christ, the Son of Abraham and David.

Time goes on with its great deeds and gentle words. The Satanic hatred of the Pharisees conspires for His destruction:—'The Pharisees went out and held a council against Him how they might destroy Him[1].' Then follows the victory of Divine gentleness. They sought to destroy: He withdrew Himself and healed[2]. If His loving eye sees one sound and living fibre in the reed, He will fill the earth with His spring, and send through the reed the sap of His grace, and save it by that fibre. If He perceives one spark in the smoking wick, He will cover it with the hollow of His hand, and breathe upon it, and waken it into a light for the feast or for the altar[3]. But the Pharisees blaspheme. 'This fellow doth not cast out devils but by Beelzebub,

---

[1] St. Matthew xii. 14. [2] Ibid. 15.
[3] Ibid. 20, cf. Isaiah xlii. 3.

the prince of the devils[1].' And judgment is pronounced,—'so it shall be also unto this wicked generation[2].'

Much more might be noticed in this connection. A little must suffice. Miracle upon miracle is wrought; yet Judaism calls for 'a sign from heaven.' There is one brief Hosanna, one fitful revival. Alas! the fig-tree (God's own type of Israel in Hosea[3],) is its image. The deceptive tree deluded the hungry by the wayside. Disciples might seek for spiritual good from a system rich in leaves, but without fruits; and so be prepared for a judgment that should blast and wither the Theocratic people from the very root. The words immediately following[4] are not hyperbole. They are prophecy. 'This mountain' is the temple-hill, the representative of Judaism; and the 'sea' into which it is to be cast and lost is the sea of nations[5]. In the twenty-second and twenty-third Chapters the great Questioner baffles

---

[1] St. Matthew xii. 24. [2] Ibid. 45.
[3] Hosea ix. 10. [4] St. Matthew xxi. 21.
[5] See Lange upon the passage.

the Sadducees and Scribes, and reduces the Pharisees to silence ; and then pours out burning words, scathing their hypocrisy and proselytism and Jesuitical distinctions. 'Ye are like unto whited sepulchres, which indeed appear beautiful outward, but are within full of dead men's bones, and of all uncleanness.' The worm of death gnaws at the foundation of Judaism. It breeds stench and pestilence. And then the true Israel went out and departed from the temple, His retreating footsteps forming the prelude to the voice which was heard afterwards,—μεταβαίνωμεν ἐντεῦθεν,—and God's Presence went with Him[1].

The same view pervades the closing Chapters.

The drama deepens to its end. He has appeared first as Law-giver; secondly, as Wonder-worker; thirdly, as Teacher. He must be more than these.—More than Law-giver. Law wakens the moral sense to obligations, towering one beyond the other into an infinite distance. Law tells the listening ear of the cruel dissonance

---
[1] St. Matthew xxiv. 1.

between the discord of that which a man is, and the perfect music of that which he ought to be. Man needs something by which he may be lifted to the distant summit; by which the sense of discord may be mitigated.—More than Wonder-worker. The miracle comes to tell us that what we call nature is not so natural after all; that man is from time to time reached by a higher law, which touches him with its light but seldom in the centuries; that He who works it has knowledge of a great chapter, whereof that which we call law is but a poor sub-section. Man wants something more than to know God's wisdom and power. —More than Teacher. The moral precept without requires a moral power within. The Parable shows us Nature with lights of God's Kingdom upon it, falling through a door which we cannot enter. Therefore, He must be more. He must be the High Priest, entering into the lowest depths; kneeling in Gethsemane, with a burden laid upon Him; hanging upon the Cross, Priest and Victim, with the pierced hands and feet, and the wounded side, and the awful circlet of the crown of thorns, and the pale and dying lips. He must then, to make this effectual, be the King reigning in glory, and sending out heralds to gather in His people, not from one race alone, but from all lands, into a Catholic Church.

We find the same conception moulding the Evangelist's materials at the close as at the beginning — accomplished Prophecy and Jewish blindness. 'The High Priest rent his clothes[1].' 'The rent garment,' says Bishop Taylor, 'signifying that the priesthood should be rent away from him and from his nation. His personated and theatric horror became the type of his punishment.' The dream of Pilate's wife and the washing of Pilate's hands are a silent but terrible reproach to the Jewish rulers[2].

This is brought out more clearly by the shapes which stand in contrast with the Chief Priests, and Scribes, and Elders, as He hangs upon the Cross. The Roman Centurion might have seen men dying on the battle-field, but never a death like that, when Jesus 'cried again with a loud

[1] St. Matthew xxvi. 65.   [2] Ibid. xxvii. 19, 24.

voice and yielded up the ghost ¹.' The women look on with pity, 'beholding afar off.' The rich man begged the Body of Jesus. But the chiefs of fallen Judaism conspire with the heathen. 'They came together unto Pilate ².' More than that, 'they gave large money unto the soldiers, saying, Say ye His disciples came by night and stole Him away, while we slept ³.' And then,—remembering doubtless how well they had succeeded with an Apostle,—in the spirit of the English Minister who said, 'every man has his price,'—and truly enough of most men whom he was likely to know,—'If this comes to the governor's ears, we will persuade him and secure you ⁴.'

Is there not prophecy there to those who will look below the surface? From that time baseness, baseness about money, has entered into the Jewish nation, and formed a leprous scurf upon it, thinned its noblest blood, and ulcerated

---

¹ St. Matthew xxvii. 50.   ² Ibid. 62.
³ Ibid. xxviii. 12, 13.   ⁴ Ibid. 14.

the hearts of the children of those who were once *homines desideriorum*. A people must act by its representatives. They may try to evade their responsibility; but, as we have seen in the last awful weeks [1], God and men will not suffer such evasion. It is full of peril to tamper with sacred things. A great nation wakens from the sleep of centuries with a stimulated conscience, and takes away, even from the altar of God, the offerings which were gathered by means which it has discovered to be unjust. With loud expressions of sorrow and pain it performs an act of national justice, which is in some sense an act of national penance. But, whatever pain may have been inflicted upon the keen susceptibility of its feelings, it has gained in the coarse material of pecuniary profit. Perhaps posterity may be ashamed to think that such undeniable advantage accompanied such ostentatious magnanimity. But, however this may be, this baseness of the Jews has become proverbial. In spite of the splendid exceptions which will occur to every

[1] Preached during the Franco-German War.

one of us, popular feeling recognises a truth in Shylock and Fagin. The base deed of fallen Judaism round the Holy Sepulchre is avenged in the wretched caricatures of the children of Abraham, who haggle with the drunken and the hungry over second-hand clothes, and sell mosaics and jewellery, the very words being a witness against them.

But enough of them. Money is not Almighty. Stones cannot keep down the Holy One, nor hierarchs suppress the living and the true. The Passion Week is ended. The Easter Sunday has come and gone. The Son of Abraham and David enters into His kingdom and passes into Galilee[1]. The spell of the mountains seems to have been on St. Matthew, and he loved to contemplate the Son of God in those solemn sanctuaries. You will remember the Mountain of the Temptation, of the Beatitudes, of the Prayer during the Storm, of the Transfiguration, and finally of the Resurrection festival. 'Then the eleven disciples went away

[1] St. Matthew xxviii. 16.

into Galilee, into a mountain, where Jesus had appointed them.' Judaism has done its worst to the bitter end. High Priests and Scribes, the heads of the ecclesiastical power, and men of the dominant theological schools; Pharisees and Sadducees, the precursors of religious parties that have lost their life, and become carrion things round which the eagles are gathering; the shadows that project themselves into the future, and become to us like familiar shapes, the Sceptic, the Jesuit, the Predestinarian, the Pharisee who is not a Protestant, and the Pharisee who is; they have killed the Holy One of God. They have wrangled and cheated, they have bribed and lied over the empty grave; but the Risen Lord is on the hills of Galilee. He is freer than the mountain air. 'All power is given unto Him in heaven and earth[1];' He sends His heralds, unconfined by the narrow limits of one land, to disciple all nations by baptizing them, and promises to be with them all days, the darkest not less than the brightest, to the end of the world[1].

[1] St. Matthew xxviii. 18, 20.

Thus does St. Matthew fill up this great conception of Prophecy accomplished in the Son of Abraham and David: of Him Who is the true Israel, in Whose work and Person true Judaism is concentrated, over against the false Judaism of a fallen priesthood and an apostate people.

II. We may now apply this view of St. Matthew's Gospel, first to the question of the origin of the Gospels, secondly in a practical way.

1. It may be looked upon as an ascertained result of criticism, that the Gospels were all written within the First Century; none earlier than about A.D. 60, none later than about A.D. 80. This historical fact will seem strange to certain modern notions. Consider for a moment how the matter really stands. Let us put ourselves in imagination back to Pentecost. In those her bridal days, the young Church was filled, not with new wine, but with a holy and heavenly enthusiasm. The light of the everlasting morning had not yet ceased to flood her spires and battlements. Her tabernacle was yet on the holy hills, and

the cry rose to her lips, 'Lord! it is good for us to be here.' With loins girded and lamps burning, she waited for her Lord's coming, and strained her eyes towards the Eternal Dawn. She was the 'Pilgrim of Eternity;' and the song which she rolled out strong and grand against the winter sky was, 'Arise we, and depart: for this is not our rest.' It may be that she had not special days of commemoration, Christmas or Good-Friday, Easter or Ascension. But she lived upon her Lord's Birth and Death, upon His Resurrection and Ascension. She needed no book of His λόγια, of His discourses, or His works. There were those with her who had seen Him on the Mountain of Transfiguration; who had heard Him say, 'Peace be unto you,' on the great Easter Sunday; and had felt joy deepening within them, as they looked upon the Atoning Wounds.

At first, then, there was not, and there needed not to be, any official memorial of the Lord. The sermons of the Apostles were in many cases summaries of our Lord's Life. Thus the whole tenor of His ministry is compressed by St. Peter into two words[1]. In portions of the Apostolic Epistles, particular incidents are mentioned or assumed. For instance, the institution of the Eucharist in the First Epistle to the Corinthians, and the Transfiguration in the Second Epistle of St. Peter. St. Paul speaks of the Birth and Circumcision of Jesus, and of His Life of poverty[2]. Other incidents of less primary importance are also alluded to in a way which implies an acquaintance with them. The writer of the Epistle to the Hebrews assumes it as 'evident,' known to all[3], that 'our Lord has arisen out of Judah.' When the same writer says, 'Jesus suffered without the gate, let us go forth, therefore, unto Him without the camp, bearing His reproach[4],' we have a reminiscence of the Saviour led out to be crucified, and of the Cyrenian bearing His cross. The 'Abba, Father' of Romans and Galatians is an echo, 'the strong crying

---

[1] $\delta\iota\hat{\eta}\lambda\theta\epsilon\nu$ $\epsilon\dot{\upsilon}\epsilon\rho\gamma\epsilon\tau\hat{\omega}\nu$, Acts x. 38.
[2] Gal. iv. 4–6; 2 Cor. viii. 9.   [3] $\pi\rho\delta\delta\eta\lambda\sigma\nu$, Hebrews vii. 14.
[4] Hebrews xiii. 13.

and tears' of Jesus in Hebrews is a scene, from Gethsemane[1]. When St. Paul desires that women 'may attend upon the Lord without distraction[2],' had he not before the eye of his mind the tender picture of the two sisters, whereof one sat at Jesus' feet, while the other was 'cumbered[3]' about much serving? In the Epistle to the Galatians the baptismal 'robing with Christ' is borrowed from the Parable of the Prodigal; it is a hint of 'Bring forth the best robe, and put it on him[4].' In the Epistle to Timothy, the Apostle urges the payment of certain Presbyters on the authority of Christ's saying, 'The labourer is worthy of his hire,' and that in a way which presupposes his knowledge of the whole discourse addressed to the Seventy[5].

---

[1] Rom. viii. 15; Gal. iv. 6; Heb. v. 7. The twelfth Chapter of the Revelation manifestly borrows its colouring from the Birth of Jesus, and Herod's 'seeking the young Child's life.' Apoc. xii. 1-4, 5.

[2] ἀπερισπάστως, 1 Cor. vii. 35.

[3] περιεσπᾶτο, St. Luke x. 40.

[4] Χριστὸν ἐνεδύσασθε, Galatians iii. 27, cf. St. Luke xv. 22.

[5] 1 Tim. v. 18, cf. St. Luke x. 7.

When St. John utters that admonition, 'He that saith he abideth in Him ought also so to walk as He made His one great life-walk [1],' whether or not we suppose that his Epistle was a circular letter accompanying the Gospel, he must have had a distinct image before his own soul, which he took it for granted was no less present to theirs. As time went on, the words of Jesus were brought to the Church's mind according to His promise. The successive needs of the Church touched and quickened the springs of memory, and events brought out the latent treasures which she possessed. 'In verbis Christi semina erant totius cursus Evangelii.' Thus, when the Holy Ghost began to fall on certain, St. Peter exclaims, 'Then remembered I the word of the Lord, how that He said, "John indeed baptized with water, but ye shall be baptized with the Holy Ghost [2]."' When St. Paul would enforce the important practical principle that the Church is not the diaphanous creature which extreme

---

[1] καθὼς ἐκεῖνος περιεπάτησε, 1 St. John ii. 6.
[2] Acts xi. 16.

Voluntaryism would make her, he remembers Christ's words, 'The labourer is worthy of his hire.' If he would remove morbid scruples from the sensitive conscience of the man who went to the entertainment of one who was external to the Church, he reminds the Corinthians how Jesus had spoken to the Seventy upon their mission, 'Eat such things as are set before you [1].' When the same Apostle deals with the question of the inviolability of the marriage bond, he falls back upon the remembered command of the Lord, 'I command, yet not I, but the Lord: Let not the wife depart from her husband'—the substance of His answer to the question of the Pharisees, 'Is it lawful for a man to put away his wife?[2]' It seems to be as certain as anything of the kind can be that an unwritten traditional Life of Jesus, graven upon the living heart of the Church, preceded the written Life. In this, startling as it seems at first hearing to some, there is no derogation from the honour of the

---

[1] 1 Cor. x. 27, cf. St. Luke x. 8.
[2] 1 Cor. vii. 10, cf. St. Matt. xix. 3, 9.

written word. No ark of the New Covenant overlaid round about with gold kept in its side the book of the New Law. There was not, as in Bacon's fine romance of Atlantis, the pillar and cross of light, breaking up and casting itself into a firmament of many stars, and the branch of palm covering the ark of cedar which floated upon the calm mysterious sea, with the volume of the Gospels shrouded in its depths. Yet the Holy Spirit guided the memories, and freely used the intelligences of Apostles and their disciples, that His Church might know the certainty of those things wherein she had been instructed; and that across the gulf of ages, and the mists of History, down to the end of time, the eyes of Christians might see the authentic lineaments of the King in His beauty.

As to the Gospel with which we are now more directly concerned, and which the Church has always attributed to St. Matthew, a denial of its authorship has been based upon the tone of the Evangelist in describing the call of St. Matthew in the ninth Chapter. 'It is impossible,' writes Schenkel, 'to conceive a colder or more impersonal narrative. It is much easier to suppose the statement in St. Luke to be his, with such a vivid touch as this, " Levi made Him a great feast in his own house¹."' The answer to such an objection is to be found in the instinctive sentiment, which made those who had stood in the presence of the All Holy One almost annihilate themselves before Him. There is a spirit which loves placard and advertisement, which multiplies tracts of which the heroes are puny or questionable saints, who write interminable experiences with eyes alternately turned to heaven, and peering to see who is listening behind the half-opened door. It was not so with Christ's Apostles. Their motto was, ' He must increase, I must decrease.' It has been beautifully conjectured that St. Matthew leaves the Parable of the Publican to be recorded by St. Luke, because *he* is the Publican from whom it was drawn. The very fact that the narrative of St. Matthew is so sober and imper-

¹ St. Luke v. 29.

sonal tells for, rather than against, its composition by the Publican who became an Apostle.

It will be observed that our analysis, so far as it is correct, establishes the unity of the authorship of this Gospel. This has been impugned by a host of modern writers. The comparatively timid Rationalism of the beginning of the Century hinted that the first two Chapters came from another hand. Ewald, twenty years ago, printed this Gospel in five different types, that the reader might have before his eyes the fragments of which it is composed. Hingelfeld assigns it to two authors,—one earlier, one later; one forcing Christianity into a Jewish mould, the other handling it in the broader spirit of St. Paul. Köstlein asserts that it was put together from three pieces, the Syro-Chaldaic original of St. Matthew, the primitive Mark, and Galilean tradition. Schenkel very similarly analyses it into a composite of a document called the 'Primitive Mark;' of a second document supposed to be spoken of by Papias as τὰ λόγια; and, added to this, of a certain amount of oral tradition.

I believe that such theories are refuted to a candid mind, even by those subordinate traits which are to a composition what the play and trick of features are to the living face, giving it individuality and character. The transitions in St. Matthew's narrative have been called by M. Réville 'simple, almost infantine.' Be it so. But the τότε, repeated more than fifty times, shows that one hand, however untutored, was at work. 'I believe,' says M. Réville again, 'that no writer ever felt happier in his work.' Certainly, the writer has throughout a simple, happy admiration for the things which he relates, and many of which he had seen. It is the same man throughout who gazes with a rapture that never tires. 'Lo!' and 'Behold!' rushes to his lips more than thirty times in this short book. The star of the Epiphany is in the East: Do you not see it? 'Lo! the star.' The Lord is on the holy mount; the cloud of glory descends upon the hill. 'Behold! there appeared unto them Moses and Elias. Behold! a bright cloud overshadowed them. Behold! a voice out of the cloud.' It is Easter Morning. The women go to tell the disciples[1], 'Behold! Jesus met them.' The Evangelist has been accused by others of being a sort of diffuse and garrulous Herodotus among the Four, passionately fond of legend and miracle. The wonders of the Infancy, the walking of Peter on the sea, the stater in the fish's mouth, the dream of Pilate's wife, the bodies of the saints reappearing after the Resurrection, the marvels at the Sepulchre, have been appealed to against St. Matthew's *credibility*; but, if they testify to his individuality, let them at least vouch for his *existence*.

Even such subordinate traits led us to the conclusion that it is one mind which addresses us. How much more must we reject the theory that this Gospel is a thin *substratum* of original writings,—beneath a stupendous layer of myths, discourses evolved out of the Church's consciousness, and agglomerated fragments of other documents,—when we perceive that the whole

[1] See the eloquent passage in M. Réville's 'Question des Evangiles.' *Revue des Deux Mondes*, June 1, 1866.

mass of the composition is not only thinly traversed by particular lines of thought, but moulded and shaped throughout by certain fundamental conceptions.

2. It remains to apply practically what has been said of this Gospel as a whole.

(*a*) There is an eternal freshness in it. Pharisees washing their hands, and making the phylactery very broad, and the tassel very long; pedantic scribes, mocking human nature with subtleties fine and glossy, but sharp and piercing as threads of glass; the haughty priests of a corrupt establishment, and its sceptical and mocking Sadducees; the wild demoniac; the publican, the man seemingly dead and buried in material pursuits, yet obeying the 'call of Jesus;' the woman of Bethany, pouring from her broken heart perfumes which were dearer to Christ than the hoarded nard; these are the shapes, 'touching and terrible,' that were never forged, which live, and speak to successive generations[1].

The spirit of hypocrisy, of Pharisaism, of hollow

[1] M. Réville, ibid. pp. 639, 640.

sanctimoniousness and hierarchical pretension, is lasting as human nature. It is scathed in St. Matthew's Gospel; no doubt of it. Only do not let us be put off by dress. We look out for the successors of Chief Priests, and Scribes, and Pharisees, in copes and chasubles, in the priest's surplice or the prelate's lawn. We may find them in other quarters, among the sentimental professors of a liberal and unsectarian Christianity, not less than among the defenders of a dogmatic creed.

Neither let us be hasty in drawing from the condemnation of formalism in St. Matthew a condemnation of forms. It is interesting to notice that the verses which put in the sharpest and clearest way the relation of the external to the spiritual element in religion are peculiar to this Gospel. '*All* the virgins,' in the parable, 'arose and trimmed their torches,' cleared the wick in the vessel, and arranged the garlands [1] around the staff which bore it; '*all* the virgins,' the wise no less than the foolish. But 'they

[1] ἐκόσμησαν, St. Matthew xxv. 7.

that were foolish took no oil; the wise took oil in their vessels with their lamps.' Christ would have neither the form without the spirit, nor the dogma without the life; neither the lamp without the oil, nor the oil without the lamp. Without the lamp, the oil will be wasted; without the oil, the lamp will not burn.

It is instructive to notice the history of that sect which, more than any other in Christendom, has professed to dispense with forms. Those excellent persons will have no bell, no organ, no spire, no painted window. The very matter of the two Holy Sacraments is offensive to them, and is idealized into types. Every believer shall be king, and priest, and offering, and altar, and temple, in one. Every life shall be a sacrifice, every day a saint's day, every meal a sacrament, every soul a church, and every throbbing heart a bell, and a liturgy, and an organ. What is the practical result? They have a hierarchy, as intolerable as ever oppressed humanity, of the most querulous and meddling of their sex, and those who really belong to them are formal in look, formal in garb, formal in the very cast of their features. The formalism and the Pharisaism, pictured and condemned in St. Matthew's Gospel, are the punishment of those who will only read one part of that Gospel.

(*b*) But that to which I would above all direct you in St. Matthew's Gospel is its representation of our Lord. If you would understand that, you must accept the theology of the text. We have indeed lately been told that 'religion and theology have no more to do with each other than an appreciation of the beauty of the Belvidere Apollo with a belief in the oracles of Delphi.' But how does this eminent philosopher define religion? That the right is wise, this, he says, is morality. That it is also loveable and beautiful, this, he says, is religion. He, therefore, who has learned to combine the sentimental admiration for virtue of Shaftesbury with the colder calculations of the utilitarian school of ethics, is religious as well as moral. But with us it is not so. Religion has for its object not a beautiful idea, but a Divine Person. Religion has for its accompaniment not a mystic rapture in the contemplation of virtue, but the action of faith that stretches out to Him from our feebleness, and the utterance of worship that speaks to Him, now in the spontaneous familiarity of prayer, now in the sublimer accents of praise. And that which is revealed of Him is not *denominationalism* which may or may not be taught. It is part and parcel of Christianity. It is not a dense theological fog obscuring the significance of the ethical ideal of Christianity; it is the substance, without which the ideal melts away. The priest who preaches a free and undenominational religion writhes in the strong garb of the more thorough-going philosopher. You read the first verse of St. John or St. Matthew. Did or did not St. John teach that the Word was God? Did or did not St. Matthew teach by the word Jesus, the Human Personality; by the word Christ, the threefold Office; by the two together, the Godhead and Manhood, with its gifts of Union and Unction? If they did, then these propositions are formulæ: and indeed it *is* childish 'to allow that the formulæ *a b c d* may be taught, only not gathered together into a formulary.'

Brethren, it is this first Verse that gives such fulness of significance to all this Gospel. It is because He is Jesus Christ, Son of Abraham and David, that His Discourses are what they are—everlasting, powerful, the inner law of Christian society and civilization, the creative source of new courage, new thoughts, new enterprises, new Saints, new Apostles, new Martyrs. This Gospel is not the life of a dead man. It is the specimen of an Eternal Life manifested upon earth for a while, by which we came to know in some measure what He is Who is our Lord. This is why it is that to leave off reading the daily lesson or chapter is to forget Christ, and with Him home and goodness. This is why men who come back to Oxford in the evening of their days, as they look back with bitter self-accusation, remember that the time which they most deplore coincided exactly with the time when, by shutting up their New Testament, they shut out Christ's Presence from their lives. Yet, thank God, we know Him, or we may know Him. We may know Him as the leper knew Him; as Peter did, when with the spray in his hair, and the storm-light on his face, he cried, 'Lord! save me;' as Galilee knew Him, when He went about doing good. Still above the clouds that hang over the Church and the world (as they hang in this land over a distracted Church, and abroad over a world in agony,) He is the Light, the Dawn and Morning Star of each new era, until the final Revelation, when, over the last clouds going up from a burning world, the Sign shall appear. Still the shadow of the Man of Sorrow hangs over the sick. Still worship is the dialogue between Him and the soul which He has redeemed with such a price[1]. Still as we kneel at the Holy Communion Sunday after Sunday, or in the stillness of the room where our dear ones lie, the Eucharist of the Upper Chamber is with us, as it was with those who heard and saw Him. Still those words are comfortable as of old, 'Come unto Me all ye that labour and are heavy laden, and I will give you rest.'

[1] See Pressensé, 'Vie de Jésus,' in the closing pages.

SERMON II.

ST. MARK.

St. Mark i. 1.

The beginning of the Gospel of Jesus Christ, the Son of God.

I HAVE examined, on a previous occasion, the fundamental ideas, the leading conceptions, of the Gospel according to St. Matthew. I shall now attempt to deal, from a similar point of view, with the Gospel of St. Mark.

I. We may be allowed to regret that St. Augustine should have spoken of St. Mark as if he were simply the 'pedissequus et breviator' of St. Matthew[1]. It may be useful, in the first instance,

---

[1] 'De Consensu Evangel.' i. 2. J. J. Griesbach stands at the head of a long list of critics who have tried to prove that the whole of St. Mark's Gospel is made up

THE LEADING IDEAS, ETC. 37

to bring together certain words of our Lord, and certain incidents in His ministry, which are peculiar to St. Mark. We shall then be able to decide whether the second synoptical Evangelist is merely the epitomizer of St. Matthew.

1. Without the Gospel according to St. Mark, the Church would have lost these among other sayings of Jesus.

We should not have possessed the great axiom (the safeguard at once against superstition and irreverence in regard to all positive institutions whatever), 'The sabbath was made for man, not man for the sabbath[1].' The two great words would be away, 'Peace, be still[2]!' Something surely would be wanting to the Parables, if we had lost that exquisite illustration of the development of God's kingdom; the seed growing, not mechanically or in virtue of cultivation, but

---

out of St. Matthew and St. Luke. It must not be forgotten that others maintain that Mark wrote the original Gospel, and was followed by Matthew and Luke. Dank, 'Hist. Revelat.' Div. iv. 279, 280.

[1] St. Mark ii. 27. [2] Ibid. iv. 39.

from within outwardly, by the energy of its hidden life [1]. Here, too, we see one ray of moral light, falling upon the corruption from which the fastidious imagination turns away sickened [2]. Here, again, in its fullest and most emphatic form, stands that saying which has nerved so many of God's children to face the syllogism, the epigram, and the scaffold. In St. Luke, 'Whosoever shall be ashamed of Me and Mine [3];' in St. Mark, 'Whosoever shall be ashamed of Me and of My words, in this adulterous and sinful generation [4].' In this Gospel only, the closing words of Isaiah are taken up and thrice repeated, 'Where their worm dieth not, and the fire is not quenched.' Here alone occurs that awful image, taken at once from the Jewish ritual, and from the realm of nature. The Judge of mankind tells us that as every offering was offered with salt, so every human soul must be seasoned by the flame of self-sacrifice and sancti-

---

[1] St. Mark iii. 26, 29.
[2] καθαρίζον πάντα τὰ βρώματα, St. Mark vii. 19.
[3] Τοὺς ἐμούς, St. Luke ix. 26.   [4] St. Mark viii. 38.

fied suffering, or by that of wrath; that it must be bathed in heavenly fire, or preserved undying in the fire of hell. 'Every one shall be salted with fire, and every sacrifice shall be salted with salt[1].' Peculiar to St. Mark's version of the discourse upon the last things, is that sudden reiterated note as of a trumpet, or tolling as of a bell, 'Take ye heed, watch ye therefore, watch and pray, watch[2].' In the same connection we must not forget three memorable words. He Who in the unity of that undivided Person is God and Man, sometimes speaks as if (to use human language) He forgot that He was not in Heaven, looking upon all things in the calmness of the perfect and eternal Light: sometimes, again, as if earth were indeed His home for a season, as if His prospects were bounded for a while by our lower horizon. 'Of that day or hour knoweth none, neither angel in heaven, *nor the Son*, but the Father only[3].' Let it not be forgotten that the word of commendation is found in these pages exclusively, which, even within the last

[1] St. Mark ix. 44, 50.   [2] Ibid. xiii.   [3] Ibid. ver. 32.

few years, dwelt as a burning fire in one woman's heart[1], enabling her to persevere in a work for the pauper-sick, which will never pass away, 'She hath done what she could[2].' Here also we find the definite prediction to St. Peter, 'Even in this night, before the cock crow twice[3].'

2. Nor can the incidents peculiar to the Gospel fairly entitle us to say of St. Mark, *solus ille perpauca.*

Those incidents are the following:—

The second Adam with the wild beast in the wilderness, while the whole forty days are filled up with one long silent suggestion of the evil one[4]; His mother and brethren taking steps to arrest Him, on the score of ecstatic absorption[5]; His sleeping in the storm on the pillow[6]; that one ray of light in the other storm, 'He *saw them* toiling in rowing[7];' the restoration of the deaf man with an impediment in his speech, and

---

[1] Agnes Jones.   [2] St. Mark xiv. 8.   [3] Ibid. ver. 30.
[4] Ibid. i. 13.   [5] Ibid. iii. 21, ὅτι ἐξέστη.
[6] Ibid. iv. 38.   [7] Ibid. vi. 48.

of the blind man of Bethsaida[1]; His design of remaining hidden in a house; His return to the sea of Galilee; the disciples having one loaf with them in the ship[2]; the history of His work along the Gaulonite range, east of Jordan; His speaking openly the sayings about His Passion[3]; the sudden disappearing of the heavenly visitants from the Mount of Transfiguration, 'the questioning one with another what the rising from the dead should mean,' the awe of the multitude at the yet unfaded brightness of His countenance[4]: the loving displeasure against the disciples who forbade the little children to come to Him[5]; the not suffering any vessel to be carried through the Temple[6]; the breaking of the alabaster box in the noble extravagance of love[7]; the emphatic record that all drank of the Eucharistic cup[8]; the repetition of the words in Gethsemane[9]; the young man, probably St. Mark himself, who left the

---

[1] St. Mark vii. 32 sqq.; viii. 22 sqq.
[2] Ibid. vii. 24, 31; viii. 14.   [3] Ibid. viii. 32.
[4] Ibid. ix. 8, 10, 15.   [5] Ibid. x. 14.   [6] Ibid. xi. 16.
[7] Ibid. xiv. 3.   [8] Ibid. ver. 23.   [9] Ibid. ver. 39.

linen cloth, and fled away naked[1]; the High Priest standing in the midst[2]; Peter beneath in the palace[3]; the first crowing of the cock[4]; the bowing of the soldiers' knees in mockery[5]; the names of the sons of the Cyrenian[6]; and, finally, the special appearance to Mary Magdalene after the Resurrection[7].

In bringing together these sayings of our Lord, or incidents in His life, which are peculiar to St. Mark's Gospel, I have no wish to evade the fact that, in the first three Evangelists, there is a certain common basis of similar—or identical—sentences, words, and even formulæ.

This common element has been differently accounted for.

By some it has been explained on the ground that the Synoptics used a common document, or documents. These, we are told, were the λόγια or Discourses, and a thin original edition of the second Evangelist, the 'Proto-Mark,' or *Ur*

---

[1] St. Mark xiv. 51. [2] Ibid. ver. 60. [3] Ibid. ver. 66.
[4] Ibid. ver. 68. [5] Ibid. xv. 19. [6] Ibid. ver. 21.
[7] Ibid. xvi. 9.

Marcus of certain German critics. The variations, according to some, are simply like the variations of musicians improvising on a given theme. The school of Tübingen gives them another origin. St. Matthew writes to refute St. Paul; St. Luke issues a Pauline manifesto. Incidents of the great Life before which ages have bowed down and worshipped, are the misunderstood inuendoes and manœuvres of 'theological diplomacy.' Texts which to the eyes of the weary and heavy laden, dim with tears of penitence and yearning, seem steeped in the soft light of eternal love, are rusty fragments of clumsy weapons, which were splintered in ignoble polemical squabbles.

But there is another and much more reasonable way of accounting for these common elements, these 'corpuscula Evangelicæ Historiæ.' The disciples very early linked together certain portions of their Master's life, partly by the nature of the subject-matter, partly according to historical sequence. By a process of 'natural elaboration' masses of this genuine Gospel tradition became rounded into a certain shape by the friction of constant repetition. As to the words of Jesus, their preservation need excite little surprise. No doubt there are discourses delivered from every pulpit (perhaps even from this) of which few hearers can recall a thought, or an expression, a week after they are delivered. The painted fire of their artificial rhetoric melts away like a coloured cloud. Their correct and elegant periods leave no more trace than a child's finger on the tide over which he floats. But there are other discourses which few hearers can totally forget, and which some could reproduce years afterwards. They contain true 'semina eternitatis.' They grasp the whole moral and rational nature. They charm the imagination by throwing exquisite lights upon homely places, whose marvellous capacities of beauty we never suspected. They win the child's heart within the man by a pathos which appeals to 'thoughts that lie too deep for tears.' They subdue the conscience, because they are the expression of an eternal law. They lay hold on the intellect by the exact correspondence between the idea and its investiture of words. They fasten themselves on the memory by that unaffected method, which is simply the apt distribution of a number of topics that may be referred to a common centre. Such, above all, were the words of Jesus [1]—'The words that I speak unto you,' He said, 'they are spirit, and they are life.' And the voice of sixty Christian generations answer, 'Thou hast the words of eternal life.' It is childish then to ask whether St. Matthew copied from St. Luke, or St. Luke from St. Matthew; whether Matthew is the 'primitive' of Mark, or Mark of Matthew. Even without taking into account the promise of the Spirit to 'bring all things to their remembrance whatsoever He had said unto them,' such words from such a teacher could never completely perish from the earth.

But however this question of the origin of the common element in the Synoptics is to be decided, the words and works of Christ, which have been preserved by St. Mark alone, are sufficiently

[1] See M. Godet, 'Sur l'Évangile de St. Luc.'

numerous and significant to prove that he is not a mere mechanical epitomizer of St. Matthew's Gospel.

II. We proceed to consider, in the second place, the leading conception and object of St. Mark. Some notice of his main characteristics will throw light upon these.

1. The main characteristic of this Evangelist is his vividness, that quality which an eloquent critic has thus described in a well-known living writer. 'He is great in single figures and striking episodes, but wants gradation and continuity. He sees history as it were by flashes of lightning. A single scene, a single figure is minutely photographed. Every tree and stone, almost every blade of grass, the attitude or expression of a principal figure, the gestures of a momentary passion, everything leaps into vision under that sudden glare[1].'

(*a*) If St. Matthew loves to lead us back to the

---

[1] Mr. Lowell on Mr. Carlyle, in 'My Study Windows.'

past, with St. Mark that past seems to become living. Hence he constantly uses the present tense in his narrative.

(*b*) 'Immediately[1]' is his 'catchword.' In two cases, at least, it is repeated three times in three consecutive verses. It occurs not less than forty-two times in this short book.

(*c*) The double negative is constantly found.

(*d*) When he records the language of any persons who are introduced into the narrative, it is frequently almost dramatic in its liveliness. Often, indeed, sentences preserved by him, reproduce the hurry and eagerness of the moment. We seem to hear the fluttered words, spoken with a beating heart, by one panting for breath. To select one example. 'I see men as trees walking,' may be resolved into three sentences. 'I see men.' 'I see them still and unmoving as trees.' 'I now see them walking[2].' The ἔα of the evil spirit (not 'let us alone,' but the 'alas,' the sigh of immortal anguish), the οὐά

---

[1] εὐθύς.
[2] Bishop Wordsworth on St. Mark viii. 24.

of the revilers, who pass by the sufferers on the Cross, are set down by St. Mark[1].

(*e*) Life-like details drop from his pencil, until narratives for which there are parallels in the other Synoptics, seem to be pre-eminently his. Witness the leper 'beseeching Him and kneeling down to Him[2];' the three successive tempests in the fourth and fifth Chapters,—the storm in the lake, the storm in the demoniac's soul, the storm of sorrow in the troubled hearts of a bereaved home. The narrative abounds in pictorial touches. I will remind you of these. The veil of the heavens rent over the baptism of Jesus[3]. The 'green grass' in the wilderness, and the companies disposed like garden plots[4]. In the night, upon the hill, under the vault of heaven, the brightness which surpasses art, and which Nature can only match in her aspects of most delicate beauty, 'exceeding white as snow, so as no fuller on earth can whiten them;' the

---

[1] St. Mark i. 24; xv. 29.   [2] Ibid. i. 40.
[3] Ibid. i. 10, σχιζομένους.
[4] πρασιαὶ πρασιαί, St. Mark vi. 39, 40.

epileptic boy, who wallowed groaning, and the father crying with tears, at the foot of the mountain, in the common day[1]. Jesus 'going before' the disciples on the way to Jerusalem[2]. The lowering and fallen look[3] of him who came running and knelt to Jesus, contrasted with the loving expression of the Master's face[4]. The name of Bartimæus, his casting away the garment in which he was wrapped, and springing up toward Christ[5]. The fig-tree withered upward from the roots[6]. The figure of the Lord, sitting over against the treasury, and praising her who gave the mite which has borne such accumulated interest[7]. That other picture of Him, sitting upon the Mount of Olives, over against the temple, and joining in His discourse the end of that august pile with the end of the world, in words before whose majesty the genius of Shakespeare himself, in his latest and most perfect lines, seems weak:—

---

[1] St. Mark ix. 3, 17, 18 sqq.   [2] Ibid. x. 32.
[3] Ibid.   [4] Ibid. vv. 17, 21.   [5] Ibid. ver. 46 sqq.
[6] Ibid. xi. 21.   [7] Ibid. xii. 41 sqq.

'The gorgeous towers, the cloud-capt palaces,
The solemn temples, the great globe itself,
Yea, all which it inherit, shall dissolve[1].'

Peter flinging himself into the thoughts of his sin, and sobbing long and loud[2]. The simple grandeur of the words, 'When the centurion saw that He so cried out, and gave up the ghost, he said, Truly this man was the Son of God[3].' The stone seen through the doubtful light of the earliest dawn, 'for it was very great[4].'

(*f*) Hence, also, we naturally find in St. Mark those personal traits of our Lord which could only have come from an eye-witness, or from one who writes under the guidance of an eye-witness, and reproduces his reverential love. Syro-Chaldaic words which fell from the lips of Jesus are preserved. St. Mark is the artist who has finished that perfect figure which our Church

---

[1] St. Mark xiii. 3 sqq.
[2] ἐπιβαλών, xiv. 72. This is differently explained by some. 'Drawing his mantle over his head (the oriental *Hyke*) he began to weep.'—Stanley on 1 Cor. xi. 7.
[3] St. Mark xv. 39.   [4] Ibid. xvi. 4.

places over her baptisteries. 'Having taken up the children in His arms and put His hands on them, He blesses them,' rains down blessings on them,—a word which, in the Septuagint, so rich in terms of benediction, occurs but once, and in the New Testament here only[1].

As life goes on with most of us, there are moments when the look of those we love come back upon us. Their sympathy, their grief, their noble indignation, speak to us from unforgotten features, when the curtain is drawn aside for a moment from the picture gallery of memory. A son will suddenly remember, in after years, a sigh which his father heaved, perhaps over his wilfulness or sin. This Gospel is a record of the looks and sighs of Jesus. I shall only refer to one passage because an unjust inference has been drawn from it. 'There is an expression in Mark,' says Schenkel, 'which shows that before His last entry into Jerusalem, Christ had never attended a festival there. Upon His arrival He betook Himself to the Temple and *looked round*

[1] κατευλογεῖ, x. 16.

about upon all things[1]. Therefore, until then, He had never seen the edifice at hand. But this is quite inconsistent with John, who tells us of His having driven the traders from the Temple at the very beginning of His career.' How much more truly did our Christian poet understand St. Mark:

> 'On Sunday eve, with many a palm,
>   With many a chant divine,
> It came, that eye so keen and calm,
>   Like a still lamp, far-searching aisle and shrine.'

It is not the stranger's look of curiosity, it is the anticipation of the Victim; it is the visitation of the Judge.

(*g*) More, perhaps, even than St. Luke, St. Mark ventures to tell how the Son of God *felt*, how 'He was moved with compassion;' 'perceived in His spirit;' 'looked round about with anger, being grieved;' 'called unto Him whom He would;' 'marvelled at unbelief;' 'was much

---

[1] περιβλεψάμενος πάντα, xi. 11. See Schenkel, 'Sketch of Character of Jesus,' p. 342.

displeased;' 'beholding, loved;' 'sighed deeply in His spirit.'

(*b*) Nor is this vividness merely the product of an opulent fancy. It is the consistency in details of a picture, whose central figure is 'drawn in lines of fire[1].' Those rapid and decided touches are inspired by a conviction of the love, the glory, and the strength of 'Jesus, the Son of God.' The canvas may seem to a merely critical eye to be overcrowded, the facts to be hurriedly accumulated. But if there is the hurry, there is also the glow and energy of life. There are words that flash out like the sword of God. High above all towers the one central Figure. The natural blindness and littleness of the disciples, nowhere else so fully exhibited, enhances His majesty. They who cried with fear, when the gust from the mountains which they knew so well swept the waters of the lake on which they had rocked from childhood, bring out the calmness of Him who says to wind and wave, 'Peace, be still!' In no other Evangelist does the divine

[1] Lange.

death stand out with grander elevation than in the quiet, compressed, 'tremendous, passionless simplicity' of St. Mark's narrative.

2. The influence of St. Peter upon this Gospel (attested by antiquity with one voice) may be repeatedly traced in its peculiarities. We can hear throughout the voice of the Apostle, who wrote 'Marcus, my son[1].'

(*a*) We not unfrequently find minute pieces of information, which must apparently have come from St. Peter. Most remarkable of all, however, is the humility, the self-effacement of the holy Apostle. It is striking, indeed, to compare his confession, and what follows it, in the eighth Chapter of St. Mark with the sixteenth Chapter of St. Matthew. St. Mark omits much of St. Peter's noble words, omits the marvellous attestation, omits the astonishing promise, yet gives the rebuke in its most pointed form. His accurate note of the second crowing of the cock aggravates the Apostle's guilt, because it shows that the first had failed to awaken his conscience[2].

[1] 1 St. Peter v. 13. [2] St. Mark xiv. 72.

(*b*) St. Peter's addresses, recorded in the second and tenth Chapters of the Acts, prove that this is just such a Gospel as he would have dictated or inspired. Both are direct and practical in their tendency. Both dwell mainly on the objective facts of the Gospel. Both exhibit the Lord's life as a career of active benevolence. The second Gospel is indeed an expansion of the words, 'He went about doing good[1].'

These characteristics of style and origin are well suited to bring out the leading ideas and primary object of the Gospel.

1. Its leading ideas.

(*a*) One of these is, that Jesus is Lord, not only of nature and the world of spirits, not only of storms and diseases, but of the sick, stormy, guilty, sorrowing, passionate, ignorant, yet yearning heart of man. He speaks; men are 'astonished and amazed.' He moves from place to place; wherever He goes, He is the magnet of the human soul. 'All men seek for Him.' Even when He is shrouded far in the silence of the

[1] Acts x. 38.

desert, even when He is in the house, 'He cannot be hid.' Still as He walks His way of life, rays of supernatural light stream from the sky, that is usually so cold and passionless, round the pathway of the Galilean peasant. They fear, as we all fear, when the sound of the tide of Eternity suddenly breaks upon our ear, and we see for a moment the heaving and glimmer of its awful waves. 'They fear exceedingly,' and 'are astonished with a great astonishment,' and 'are sore amazed in themselves.' As that master hand sweeps without effort the chords of the human soul, its deepest and finest tones—amazement, wonder, reverence, trust, adoration—answer to the marvellous touch.

(*b*) A second leading idea of St. Mark's Gospel is, that the Life of Jesus is a life of alternate rest and victory, withdrawal and working[1].

So, in the first Chapter, we find the retirement in Nazareth, the coming forth to be baptized; the withdrawal into the wilderness, the walk in Galilee; the rest in the cool sanctuary, where

[1] See Lange on St. Mark.

the dawn breaks upon the kneeling man, and the going forth to preach to the heated and struggling crowd. Thus, once more, the withdrawal to the Mount of Olives is followed by the great conflict of the redeeming Passion, while that is succeeded by the withdrawal into the Sepulchre. It is the book of the wars of the Lord, and the rest of the Lord. The first rest was in Nazareth; the first trophies were the four Apostles. The last rest is in the Heaven of Heavens, in 'the privacy of glorious light;' the last victory (for this great book never ended with the words 'they were afraid') is diffused over all time—'the Lord working with them, and confirming the work with signs following.'

2. As to the primary object of St. Mark's Gospel.

St. Mark addressed himself specially to the Latin element in humanity.

The origin of this Gospel was placed in Rome by Clement of Alexandria, and connected by him with St. Peter's labours in that city. Though there is no authority for the story that it was written in Latin[1] (which would not have been necessary in the early Roman Church), it contemplates the Latin race, and is addressed to Latin thought.

The second Gospel contains several Latin words[2]; some of them, as we are occasionally told with a peculiar sneer, 'somewhat imperfectly Grecized.' In one instance the names of two individuals are mentioned, who would be known to members of the Roman Church—Alexander and Rufus[3].

But we have something which lies much deeper than these superficial indications.

The Roman temperament was eminently practical. 'Their earliest character,' it has been said, 'was steady agricultural thrift. This was turned into the steady pursuit of conquest, and all by the practical method and spirit[4].' The latest writer on the subject remarks that 'the old Roman

---

[1] Appendix, Note 3.

[2] ii. 4; vi. 8; vii. 4; xii. 41, 42; xv. 16, 39, 44. Roman customs are referred to, x. 12; xiv. 30, and Jewish customs explained, vii. 1 sqq.; xii. 42.

[3] Romans xv. 21; cf. xvi. 13.   [4] Mr. Carlyle.

religion is the most practical that ever existed.' He points, in confirmation, to their worship, which was symbolical and undogmatic; to their deities, who, so far as they were of the Roman stamp, were virtues personified; to their pontiffs, who were largely charged with legal and material interests; to their Lectisternia, which were rather repasts for social union than religious banquets; to their whole idea of the gods, which was that of a hostile nation of indisputable strength[1]. There can be no doubt, however, that a considerable element of the Roman mind had begun to be honeycombed by scepticism.

In St. Mark's Gospel, accordingly, we find not so much the highest ideas explanatory of facts, as facts themselves. The whole Gospel is a commentary on one epithet, the use of which in the first line of 'In Memoriam' has been stigmatized as an affectation—'Strong Son of God!' Throughout, the notion of strength is kept in view. Never was hell stronger on earth than

[1] 'La Théocratie Romaine,' par M. Henri Rucher. *Revue des Deux Mondes*, May 15, 1871.

when Jesus taught in Galilee. There are times when the usual equilibrium of moral and spiritual life is disturbed; when we are tempted to ask, with Bishop Butler, why whole masses of men should not go mad at once; or to say with the French physician, as he looked upon a population, half of them stupefied and another half frantic, that they are seized with epidemic insanity. Such a time was that when Jesus walked upon earth. In the lurid darkness of eras like these, Satan finds a home in the seething human soul. Nowhere is the personality of evil spirits, the interpretation of the human consciousness by them, so clearly noted as by St. Mark[1]. Nowhere is Satan so emphatically the strong one,—Jesus the Stronger. But this strength is not the strength of magic with its formulæ and incantations. The second Gospel is pervaded by an intense conviction that it is His word which is so mighty. The weapon of victory is the 'New Teaching[2],' the assurance of forgiveness that pene-

---

[1] Note the masculine participle with the neuter noun, ix. 20, 26; cf. i. 22, 23; v. 2.   [2] διδαχὴ καινή, i. 27.

trates the nervous system as with an electric stream, and works from within outwardly[1]. To the Roman admiration of thought and heroism, as well as to the scepticism of its exhausted speculation, St. Mark seems to say,—Here is a plain account—so plain and straightforward that it cannot be suspected—of the words and works of Jesus Christ. You admire power, and make ambition virtue. With His calm superhuman eye, He sees through it, and knows its littleness. For Him conquerors and kings are 'they who are accounted to rule over the Gentiles'—those who seem to themselves and others to rule, while they are the slaves of irresistible circumstances and unresisted lusts[2]. Here is a holier heroism, here is a stronger strength, here is a royalty of love. Here is the victory of Him Whom one of your own rough centurions declared to be really the Son of God; Who was crowned with the twisted thorn and stood in the Prætorium, and had the faded camp-mantle of one of your soldiers flung upon Him, but is now set down at the Right

---

[1] ii. 5.   [2] οἱ δοκοῦντες ἄρχειν, St. Mark x. 42.

Hand of God, and strongly works with the Church which you see advancing to her victory.

III. From this survey we may, I think, derive an intellectual, a theological, and a personal lesson.

1. An intellectual lesson. Have we, of this age and place, anything to learn from the manner and substance of this Divine Book, as addressed to a particular age and people?

What is the present state of speculation in reference to the foundations of religious, and even moral, belief outside and inside Oxford?

(*a*) Outside Oxford.

We are told, half in pity, that 'Modern thought is a rising flood, which, if it rises high enough, will drown all the Christian congregations in their churches. Humane men take it not as a light thing, but as an almost appalling thing, that the whole mass of faithful unargumentative Christian women should have their dearest hopes of an hereafter in Heaven with their dead destroyed in a brief period of scientific lecturing[1].' I interrupt this quotation to say that I do not fully share the alarm expressed in the last sentence by this kindly sceptic. I do not think that the mass of educated Christian women are either the utterly unscientific or utterly unargumentative beings whom he supposes.

(*b*) In Oxford.

I speak, upon high authority, in saying that the students in Philosophy run some risk of having their faith shaken. Some, doubtless, think that this is a matter for little concern. They will tell us that most Oxford men, devoted to boating and cricket, riding and lounging, begin and end their Academic career in a condition of stolid English incuriousness, which they will carry back, like their respectable fathers, to the Quarter Sessions, or to the Sleepy Hollow of a country parsonage. Such persons will add that the so-called disturbance of religious convictions is a mere loosening of the crust of dogmatism or ignorance. Others will console those who have

[1] 'Pall Mall Gazette,' May 11, 1871.

calcined the statue of Divine Beauty, which they bore within their souls, in the fires of intellectual agony, by telling them that, if the marble has been precipitated into lime, they may work up the lime into some plausible likeness of the glorious thing which they have destroyed, and write its name upon the plinth. Others, thoughtful men, see a something which they confess to be alarming. Toleration, one of their number admits to be merely 'the comprehensive complacency of modern scepticism.' He dwells upon certain significant tokens in general society. He refers to the increasing use of stimulants; the pruriency of our novels; the fierce lasciviousness of a school of poetry, where intellect drives on the passions as the devils drove the swine of old; the strange and unexpected revelations of sympathy, at least, with the things that come to Christians from certain songs of Horace and Virgil, and even from the Symposium of Plato, like the sudden smell of putrefaction in a glorious garden. But all this he traces to 'the reaction among young men from Theological and Philosophical controversy, which leads them, *especially at Oxford*, to treat all varieties of religion as unlike worthy of attention from those to whom art and culture can unfold their treasures.' His emphatic conclusion is, 'That unless some non-theological basis of morals can be found, we may be pardoned for hoping that the old Theological basis may not be long in reasserting itself[1].'

If I may leave for a moment the direct line of our thought, is it over presumptuous, in presence of such facts, to express a wish that young men might be initiated into philosophy by some other method than that of Spinoza? I do not know that any philosophical teacher but Hegel has ever written over the porch of his school, 'Let no *aspinozist* enter.' 'Thought,' says Hegel[2], 'must elevate itself to the level of Spinozism before rising higher again. Do you wish to be philosophers? Begin by being Spinozists; you can do nothing without that. It is necessary, before all things, to bathe in that sublime ether

[1] 'Saturday Review,' May 20, 1871.
[2] 'History of Philosophy,' iii. 374.

of the sole, universal, impersonal substance, where the soul rejects all, absolutely all, which it has hitherto believed. You must have arrived at that negation which is the emancipation of the mind.' This oracle of Hegel being interpreted means,—Let the young man's intellect be steeped in Spinoza's idea of substance. He will then see that will, consciousness, personality, transferred from man to God, are absurdities and contradictions. He will get rid, in the most compendious way, of the childish idea of a Personal God. The man who has read Spinoza more carefully than others thus sums up his protracted study: 'Spinoza,' says M. Saisset, 'setting out from the abstract and barren principle of substance, ends at last by defacing the idea of God, and degrading that of the soul, i.e. by the overthrow of all religion and all morality. In spite of its strong and beautiful arrangement, the system of Spinoza appears to me to be a series of arbitrary premises and impious conclusions.' The conclusion of a most competent Christian philosopher in relation to Hegel is, that his system is the concentrated sophistry of ages, and that it destroys the necessary laws of reason. It destroys alike induction which finds principles, and syllogism which deduces consequences, by affirming that contradictions are identical[1].

Surely there is some reason for asking that the pantheist and the sophist should not be the first initiators of our youth in speculation, that Descartes, Newton, Liebnitz, Reid, Butler, Plato, and Aristotle should be restored to the seats from which they have been thrust down.

Doubtless the Oxford of twenty-five years ago had many deficiencies. As we look over a Calendar of that date, there are names which we associate with melancholy deaths, and lives more melancholy still. But there was one kind of tragedy which was very rare, a mental tragedy, such as that which has been related by a distinguished French thinker[2]. A student paced his room on a well-remembered night. He was

[1] Gratry, Logique du Panthéisme, Principe d'identité; Logique, i. 109, 269.   [2] Jouffroy.

following the course of his thought, piercing through layer after layer, until he should reach the lowest depth of his consciousness. He flung from him one illusion after another. He clung to the last relic, as the swimmer clings to his plank. Shuddering at the unknown around him, with its cold waters and voices moaning in the dreadful distance, he feebly pushed back towards the shore which he had left, back to the home of childhood, back to the village church, back to the prayer of faith, back to the thought of life beyond the grave, back to the Cross that was not yet robbed of a Redeemer, to a Heaven that was not yet untenanted of the living God. But the tide was too strong for the swimmer, and sucked him further out from the shore, where his heart would be. The long self-questioning came to an end. Nothing was left to him of the heritage of his faith. Then the old life, full of hope and innocent laughter, died out; and before him lay another, dark and lonely, where he must walk, with the fatal thought, which he cursed while it fascinated him! Oxford men of the time to which I refer might have much to regret bitterly. But at least, as a general rule, they had not lost the very elements of belief. The Sacrament had not been deprived of its presence and of its gift. Heaven was something more than an illusion of air and light. Those who had fallen asleep in their arms, with the tears of love upon their cold faces, had not gone down in a sea that could never give up its dead. Faith and penitence had not withered from the very roots. The touch of the Spirit might yet quicken them into life.

To an age, then, and to men resembling those whom the second Evangelist addressed, in being partly material, partly sceptical, appreciating keenly, however, that which is effective, Christ should be preached, with strong, grave, plain, manly, historical simplicity. We should follow St. Mark, as he lifts up his finger and points to a long succession of trophies over human misery and sin; to that glorious compassion which raised those who were fallen upon the field of life; to the sufferer dying, as one of old said, so lordly;

to the Victor at God's right hand, Whose mighty presence is with His Church, and enables her to fill the earth with the spirit of His words and the continuation of His works. There may be something beyond evidences of Christianity in the self-evidence of the Gospel of Jesus Christ, the Son of God.

2. The second lesson which I would draw from our survey is a Theological one.

The text, and indeed the whole of St. Mark, shows us what the Gospel is.

The word Gospel occurs in the New Testament more than seventy times. The underlying idea is always glad news, or joyful communication. A common view of hearing the Gospel is this: A man has been so unhappy as never to have listened to a faithful preacher up to a certain time. Then first he hears of God's eternal purpose, of an effectual calling by His Spirit working in due season, of conversion, of assurance, of perseverance. He feels uplifted from the lower earth, and set upon the rock that is higher than man. He cries aloud with joy. He is safe, because he knows that he is safe.

Now let me not be misunderstood. I, for one, will not speak lightly of statements, some of which are not only the stay and comfort of loving hearts, but which are eternally true, while others are only exaggerations of blessed and eternal truths. But be they true or be they false, or partly true and partly false or exaggerated, yet, as a matter of fact, they are not the Gospel— not that which the New Testament calls the Gospel. For the New Testament Gospel is this. The glad news that for us sinners, and for our salvation, the Word of God has taken the Manhood into God; taken the Body, framed and moulded by the Eternal Spirit, to be the meet habitation of the Word; for us come upon earth; for us lived; for us wrought miracles; for us died upon the accursed Tree; for us broken the prison-bars of the tomb; for us ascended; for us sent down the Holy Spirit.

I might appeal to the opening of the Epistle to the Romans, to the almost formal definition of the Gospel in the beginning of the fifteenth chapter of the First Epistle to the Corinthians, to the structure and character of the four Gospels. But I need little proof beyond our text. The word Gospel is a favourite word with St. Mark. In commenting upon the text, Bengel observes that 'the *beginning* of the Gospel is in the Baptist, the *Gospel* in the whole book.' But what Gospel? Simply the events from the Baptism of Jesus to His Death and Ascension.

Now, if this be the true idea of the Gospel, let us be assured that the Church preaches not this or that fragment of it, but the whole Gospel, fully and unceasingly. By her great days of observance, by the Christian seasons, we have a living, permanent, continuous preaching of the Gospel, as St. Mark understood the word, taken up into the structure and texture of our lives, diffused round the circling year, emphasized by the festivities of home, borne into our hearts with the chiming of the Parish Church bells. And this is reinforced by a daily recounting in the Creed of those facts which are the

Gospel, by our daily and Eucharistic worship, and by our fixed standards of doctrine.

I believe that this has a direct bearing on the question of the duty of maintaining an Established Church. I am not prepared to assert that certain arguments commonly adduced in this controversy are sound. I do not, for instance, believe that a Church like the English Church can ever be starved. For, with a dexterity improved by practice in that which was once thought sacrilege, financiers can now easily produce a scheme of commutation which may do enough to give illiberal Churchmen an excuse for doing nothing. The high pressure of the rivalry of competing religious republics would, no doubt, make a wide religious provision of some sort.

The downfall of the Establishment need not be the downfall of Christianity. But for generations Christianity might be dwarfed and belittled, so far as human perversity can affect that which is divine. The Church might be a tent to be taken down and reared up again, not a cathedral, with glorious figures carven upon unearthly pillars, and the stars resting upon its tall pinnacles. The city might remain, but it might be vulgarised by tumultuous occupants. The frogs might come up, yea, into the chambers that once were tenanted by the kings of thought. In England you have many democrats and many sciolists. But, as yet, you are happy enough to know little of the theological democrat, and the theological sciolist. It might be that truth would ultimately prevail, though there is no promise to individual churches. It might be that agitation would be the storm on which brave hands should fling out the banner of truth, in broader and brighter folds. But, for a time at least, if we may judge from the scanty records of Disestablishment, there would be danger to something more than 'the drawing-room precedence of the Vicar,' or the spiritual peerage of the Bishop, even to the fulness and perfection of the Gospel of Jesus Christ, the Son of God.

3. A personal lesson.

The figure which stands out from this book is Jesus. It is the Gospel of Jesus Christ, the Son of God.

A man must be holy to comprehend the holiness of Jesus.

Let us suppose the case of a sharp man, who has neither taste nor genius, standing before a great picture; he will point out flaw after flaw in Raphael. Place one who has neither musical appreciation, nor modesty to admit it, where he must hear Beethoven. It is an unmeaning noise, which gives him a headache. Even so, the lower the moral and spiritual life may be, the less is Jesus understood and loved. To an easy, soft-mannered, hard-hearted man of the world; to a subtle, bitter, selfish scholar, with the delicate intellectual egotism, and the fatal gift of analysis *à outrance*, Gethsemane and the Cross may be a scandal or a mockery. The Gospel, which seems so poor and pale when we rise from the songs of poets and the reasonings of philosophers, is a test of our spirit. Let some ambitious students in philosophy — some who have been communing for hours with the immortal masters of history, charmed with the balanced masses and adjusted perspectives of the composition, speak out their mind to-day upon this Gospel of St. Mark. They will not place it very high upon their list. But turn to it to-morrow, when the end of your toil finds you disappointed men; when, after the examination, the curtain falls upon the tragedy of the Class-list; when sorrow visits you; when, as you put your hand upon the wall of your room, memory, like a serpent, starts out and stings you. Then you will recognise the infinite strength and infinite compassion of Jesus. Out of your weakness and misery, out of your disappointment, (for Oxford is always setting up kings whom it soon dethrones)—you will feel that here you can trust in a nobility that is never marred, and rest that tired heart of yours upon a love that never fails, in the Gospel of Jesus Christ, the Son of God.

On the whole, then, in St. Mark we have not so much as in St. Matthew, the point of convergence of the prophetic rays in the Messiah, the Son of Abraham and David. Not so much as in St. Luke, the fairest of the children of men,

Priest and Victim, the Teacher of grace and forgiveness. Not so much as in St. John, the Eternal Word made Flesh, floating in a robe of heavenly light. It is the Gospel whose emblem is the Lion, whose Hero is full of divine love and divine strength. It is the Gospel which was addressed to the Romans to free them from the misery of scepticism, from the grinding dominion of iron superhuman force unguided by a loving will. Here, brief as it is, we have, in its essential germs, all the theology of the Church. Had every other part of the New Testament perished, Christendom might have been developed from this. A man's faith does not consist of the many things which he affects to believe or finds it useful to believe, (as men are said to be doing in France), but of the few things which he really believes, and with which he stands, fronting his own soul and eternity. This faith in the Gospel of Jesus Christ, the Son of God, is sufficient. Hold it fast, and you shall find the power of one of our Lord's promises which is peculiar to this Gospel. If you are called upon to 'handle the serpents' or 'to drink the deadly things[1]' of science and philosophy, you shall lift up the serpent as a standard of victory. The cup of poison shall not reach your heart as it reached the heart of Socrates, when the sun was going down behind the hill tops[2]. 'It shall not hurt you.' Hold fast this Gospel in that which tries many who are undisturbed by speculative doubt, in conscious sinfulness, in the allurements of lust. Hold it fast in the din of voices that fill a Church distracted by party-cries, and 'He who has instructed His Church by the heavenly doctrine of His Evangelist St. Mark, will grant that, being not like children carried away by every blast of vain doctrine, you shall be established in the truth of His holy Gospel.'

[1] St. Mark xvi. 18.
[2] Lange and others have supposed that our Lord's words may contain this allusion. See the Phædo of Plato.

SERMON III.

ST. LUKE.

St. Luke i. 3.

It seemed good to me also, having had perfect understanding of all things from the very first, to write unto thee in order, most excellent Theophilus.

We have laid it down as a principle, that the Evangelists do not profess to give complete biographies of the earthly life of our Lord. Each, having his materials before him, moulds and arranges them according to certain leading thoughts, certain fundamental conceptions. The attempt to ascertain these is our present task.

This morning I take for my subject the leading thoughts of the third of the synoptical Evangelists, leaving St. John for other occasions.

I. It is no part of my design to attempt anything like a biography of the Evangelists. But the peculiar points of view in St. Luke are so much directed by his personal history, that I must recall two circumstances to your recollection.

1. St. Luke was a Gentile.

This would seem to follow from two passages in the fourth Chapter of the Epistle to the Colossians[1]. Aristarchus, Marcus, Jesus Justus were 'of the circumcision.' Therefore Epaphras, Luke, and Demas were Gentiles. 'The Jews were put in trust with the oracles of God[2],' and through them, with the one great exception of the author of the third Gospel and of the Acts of the Apostles, they were all delivered.

2. Though not converted by St. Paul, who never speaks of Luke as 'his son,' the Evangelist was much with the Apostle of the Gentiles. We do not, of course, confound Luke with Lucius, St. Paul's kinsman[3]. But there is ample evidence of their companionship. The narratives of St. Paul's journeys, in the Acts of the Apostles, frequently run in the first person plural, '*we*.' This first appears in the sixteenth Chapter of Acts[4],

---

[1] iv. 10, 11; cf. 12, 14. [2] Romans iii. 2.
[3] Λοῦκας, Col. iv. 14; Λούκιος, Rom. xvi. 21. [4] xvi. 10.

where, after the third person frequently repeated in the previous verses, the expression occurs, 'we endeavoured to go into Macedonia.' It has been conjectured that, as there were hot springs at Troas, which attracted many sick persons, St. Luke's profession, as a physician, may have been exercised there. Every one, of course, knows that it has been suspected by those critics, who in the name of plain common sense weave theories of almost superhuman subtlety, that these passages are fragments of a narrative, drawn up by some other companion of St. Paul, intercalated by the author of the Acts, and therefore no proof that St. Luke himself ever made these voyages. The most natural view, surely, is that the writer was one of the company. But, however this may be, two passages in St. Paul's Epistles attest his familiarity with St. Luke. 'Only Luke is with me,' writes the Apostle in one place [1]. And again, in the Epistle to Philemon [2], Lucas is mentioned among St. Paul's 'fellow-labourers.'

[1] 2 Timothy iv. 11.   [2] συνεργοί Philemon ver. 24.

II. Let us see whether these two facts have not left an unmistakeable impress upon the leading ideas of St. Luke's Gospel.

But, first, lest we should seem to lose a fact in the pursuit of an idea, let us notice that St. Luke professes to write, καθεξῆς, ἀκριβῶς, ἄνωθεν[1]. Of the three notions conveyed by the word καθεξῆς (*temporal, local,* and *logical*), the first is commonest with St. Luke, in whom alone among the New Testament writers the word is to be found. 'St. Luke,' says Tischendorf, 'thus professes to write the Life of Christ with historical accuracy, i.e. preserving the order of events where it seemed necessary.' Three facts confirm this interpretation: (1) that certain chronological marks are given by St. Luke alone[2]; (2) that the narrative is made to fall into certain temporal limits, and especially, according to Jewish use, into weeks[3]; (3) that he occasionally intimates that the exact order is either unknown to him, or left undetermined by him.

---

[1] St. Luke i. 1–4. [2] Ibid. ii. 1; iii. 1, 23.
[3] σάββατα.

I return to the bearings of these facts of St. Luke's life upon his Gospel.

1. St. Luke was a Gentile.

(*a*) Hence one leading idea of his Gospel is the rejection of the Jews. This idea breathes sadly through Simeon's Song: 'This child is set for the fall and rising again of many in Israel[1],' the first hint of opposition from unbelief which occurs in this Gospel. It appears in St. Luke's account of the Baptist's terrible words, not only as in St. Matthew 'to the Pharisees and Sadducees,' but to 'the multitude that came forth to be baptized of him, O generation of vipers! the axe is laid unto the root of the trees[2].' It pervades the close of our Lord's Discourse in the synagogue at Nazareth[3]. It is typified in that first rejection of the Holy One, when He was led to the brow of the Mount of Precipitation, the first prelude of another more tragic and final[4]. It gives solemn pathos to those words of the

---

[1] St. Luke ii. 34.
[2] Ibid. iii. 7, 9.
[3] Ibid. iv. 25, 27.
[4] Ibid. iv. 29.

weeping Saviour, 'Because thou knewest not the time of thy visitation[1].

(*b*) This Gentile Evangelist, possibly writing his Gospel from Rome, the capital of the Gentile world, and impressed with the rejection of the Jews, brings before us the Gospel as the Gospel of Humanity, the Saviour as the Saviour of the world. 'It forms,' says Schenkel, 'the Gentile-Christian antithesis to the Jewish Christian thesis in the evangelical history, and it aims to give Christianity an universal significance.' 'According to the preface, it is a composition intended to confirm the faith of a distinguished Gentile catechumen in evangelical truth.' Born in a stable, under the Roman Emperor, He who was conceived by the Holy Ghost and born of the Virgin Mary is the Saviour of all men. His genealogy is brought up to Adam, the head of our Humanity, not to Abraham, the progenitor of the Jewish people[2]. While St. Matthew speaks chiefly of the Twelve as representatives of the twelve tribes, St. Luke lays more stress upon the sending

---

[1] St. Luke xix. 44.   [2] Ibid. iii. 38.

of the Seventy, that number being the symbol of the nations under the Theocracy[1]. The great episode of the so-called 'Journey Report[2]' mentions a journey through Samaria to Judæa and Jerusalem. We may note in it tenderness to the Samaritans, in refusing to bring down fire from heaven[3], and in choosing the Samaritan as the embodiment of charity in that story[4] whose beauty has never been exceeded but by another, 'of which Jesus is not the narrator but the subject.' Note, too, that breathing of deathless hope over Tyre and Sidon, 'if the mighty works had been done in Tyre and Sidon, which have been done in you, they had a great while ago repented[5].' And, above all, the Parables of the Lost Sheep and the Prodigal Son, which touch upon the exile and the return of God's self-banished children with such tender and tearful love.

2. St. Luke was much with St. Paul. Ancient writers attributed a Pauline colouring and influ-

---

[1] Cf. St. Luke ix. 1, 6; x. 1, 20.
[2] Ibid. ix. 51; xviii. 30.
[3] Ibid. ix. 51, 56.
[4] Ibid. x. 30, 37.
[5] Ibid. ver. 13.

ence to St. Luke's Gospel, as much as a Petrine to St. Mark's. So much so, indeed, that some of them have asserted, not only that 'the brother, whose praise is in the Gospel¹,' is St. Luke as its author, but that St. Paul refers to it when he speaks of ' my Gospel².'

Before noticing the connection between this Pauline influence and one of the pervading ideas of St. Luke's Gospel, let me remind you of some less prominent, yet surely most important, traces of it.

One of the most interesting passages in the New Testament is the account of the institution of the Holy Communion, in the eleventh Chapter of First Corinthians. It contains the earliest record of the Eucharist, the earliest written words of our Lord. We find a remarkable coincidence with this in St. Luke's narrative, more especially in one point. St. Matthew and St. Mark say of the Bread, εὐλογήσας, of the Cup, εὐχαριστήσας. St. Luke alone says of the Bread,

---

¹ 2 Cor. viii. 18.
² Rom. ii. 16; xvi. 25; 2 Tim. ii. 8.

εὐχαριστήσας, and in this he coincides with St. Paul[1].

Few words are more familiar to all students than χάρις and πίστις. Χάρις occurs about one hundred and forty-six times in the New Testament, only on twenty-one occasions outside St. Paul's and St. Luke's writings; πίστις is found in some two hundred and forty-three places, not quite fifty-three times outside St. Paul and St. Luke.

All readers of St. Paul's Epistles must have been arrested by the contrast drawn in the fifth of Romans and the fifteenth of First Corinthians, between the first man, who is from the earth, of dust, and the Second Man, whose origin is from Heaven[2]. Is not the germ of this great thought in the last clause of the Genealogy in the

---

[1] St. Matthew xxvi. 26, 27, λαβὼν τὸν ἄρτον, καὶ εὐλογήσας ... λαβὼν ποτήριον καὶ εὐχαριστήσας. So St. Mark xiv. 22, 23. But in St. Luke xxii. 19, 20, λαβὼν ἄρτον εὐχαριστήσας, κ.τ.λ. Cf. 1 Cor. xi. 24, εὐχαριστήσας ἔκλασεν.

[2] ἐκ γῆς χοϊκός (cf. χοῦν ἀπὸ τῆς γῆς, Gen. ii. 7), ὁ δεύτερος ἄνθρωπος ἐξ οὐρανοῦ. See Tischendorf, and Reiche, Comm. Crit. 1 Cor. xv. 47.

third Chapter of St. Luke, 'which was the son of Adam, which was the son of God'?

Once more. Abused as it may have been by fanaticism, is not the hope of the restoration of Israel in accordance with Scripture? Jerusalem is dear to every man of the race of Israel. The celebrated writer who is accused by his enemies of metaphysical glitter, of exaggerated tinsel and affected antithesis, becomes serious when he speaks of her. His description of Jerusalem is drawn with the pencil of a genuine enthusiasm. We feel that the anticipation of prophecy elevates his style when he rejoices in the fact that the terraced gardens are again ascending the hills of Jerusalem; that 'the true children of the land, the vine and the olive,' are again exulting in their native soil. Is not the thought of Israel's restoration in the words, preserved by St. Luke, 'They shall be led away captive into all nations; and Jerusalem shall be trodden down of the Gentiles, until the times of the Gentiles be fulfilled'[1]? What footsteps of suc-

---
[1] St. Luke xxi. 24.

cessive armies, Roman, Saracen, Crusader, Turk, must have risen in His ear, who thus spoke! The sole parallel to this passage is in the eleventh Chapter of St. Paul's Epistle to the Romans.

I have remarked these isolated coincidences, betwen St. Paul and St. Luke, because they seem to give more prominence to one of the great leading ideas of St. Luke's Gospel, which is also the leading idea of St. Paul; which, therefore, he did not develope from any other source than the Life and words of Christ.

What aspect of the Redeemer's work is most present to St. Paul? What note of the trumpet is it that thrills us most? Forgiveness, pity, grace. 'Non gratia ex operibus, sed opera ex gratia.'

This is throughout a fundamental conception of St. Luke, in those passages which are peculiar to him. All is Christ's gift. So is it with the lower blessings of healing. 'Unto many that were blind He *gave* sight [1].' So much more with the higher gift of pardon and peace. Does not

---
[1] ἐχαρίσατο βλέπειν, St. Luke vii. 21.

this apply to the story of the sinful woman who anointed the feet of Jesus; to the Parables of the love of God the Son in seeking the lost, and of God the Father in going to meet the prodigal, when he is yet a great way off[1]? Consider, again, the Parable of the Pharisee and Publican[2], probably not recorded by St. Matthew, because *he* might be supposed to be the Publican from whom it was drawn. In an age which must have outrageous excitement, people run after the converted prize-fighter, or to hear the life, babbled out in a sermon, of some poor sinner with the rouge scarcely washed from her faded face. So was it not with St. Augustine in his Confessions, where the mother of his lost Adeodatus passes into the silence, veiled and tearful, a shadow without a name. So was it not with Apostles. Nor shall we fail to remark in this Parable of the Pharisee and the Publican the word which we have learned to associate with St. Paul's writings, *Justification*[3]. The same thought

---

[1] St. Luke vii. 36 sqq.; xv.   [2] Ibid. xviii. 10 sqq.
[3] Ibid. ver. 14.

appears in section after section. We shall at once remember Zaccheus, to whose home salvation comes, for the Son of Man came to seek and to save that which was lost; the look that recalled Peter to himself; the word from the Cross, preserved by St. Luke, 'Father, forgive them, for they know not what they do;' that other word to the dying thief, who believed that in the pierced Hands lay the keys of death and hell, 'To-day shalt thou be with me in Paradise;' the commission that 'Repentance and remission of sins should be preached in His name among all nations, beginning at Jerusalem[1].'

This Gospel, whose key-note and leading idea is forgiveness; which has, as its own peculiar treasures, the forgiveness of the fallen woman, of the Publican, of the crucifiers, of the dying Thief, of a world if that world will receive it; comes well from the Gentile Evangelist, the friend of St. Paul the great Doctor of Grace, who wrote his Gospel under St. Paul's guidance and encou-

---

[1] St. Luke xix. 9, 10; xxii. 61; xxiii. 34, 43; xxiv. 47.

ragement. It is interesting to find the results of independent criticism agreeing with the oldest Church tradition as represented in the ancient fragments of the Muratorian Canon. That part of the Canon which refers to St. Luke's Gospel is thus interpreted by Credner and Gieseler:—' The third book of the Gospels, that according to St. Luke. This Luke, the Physician, after Christ's Ascension, St. Paul had taken with him as a seeker after righteousness. This Gospel, according to general opinion, bore the name of Luke, though really Paul's.'

Such are the leading ideas of St. Luke's Gospel. It is written with a nearer approach to chronological sequence than the rest. It is pervaded by the thought of the rejection of the Jews. It exhibits the Saviour as the Saviour of the World. It is the Gospel of free grace, of free and abounding pardon. So true is the saying of one of old that 'as the Apostles were made from fishers, fishers of men, so St. Luke, from a physician of bodies, was made a physician of souls.'

III. I should ill have succeeded in conveying to your minds even such an impression as this Gospel leaves upon my own, if I did not refer to two other great characteristics which it possesses.

1. St. Luke is eminently the psychologist among the Evangelists. He was, as we know, a physician. Perhaps we may trace this in his tone of speaking of their art—'which had spent all her living upon physicians, neither could be healed of any,'—compared with the severer words of St. Mark, 'and had suffered many things of many physicians, and had spent all that she had and was nothing bettered, but rather grew worse[1].' We can scarcely doubt that the beautiful saying preserved by him in common with the other Synoptics, 'They that are whole need not the physician, but they that are sick,' must have been specially affecting to one who had himself been a physician[2]. Certainly we find throughout that symptoms of diseases were more carefully described by one who had been trained to observe them,

---

[1] St. Luke viii. 43; cf. St. Mark v. 26.
[2] St. Matthew ix. 12; St. Mark ii. 17; St. Luke v. 31.

and who, though he could neither have been a disciple of our Lord, nor an eye-witness, was thus prepared to understand many of the miracles better. You will easily recall Simon's mother 'taken with a great fever;' the sick brought to Him when the sun was setting; the man 'full of leprosy;' the clear discrimination between those who were afflicted with diseases, and those who were possessed; the joining of the healing the sick with the preaching of the Kingdom of God. Add to which that the last miracle of healing is recorded by St. Luke alone. 'And He touched his ear and healed him [1].'

The physician is, perforce, something of a psychologist. This may arise from the mysterious connection between mind and body, and from the opportunities which he possesses of observing the subtler traits of many temperaments in the hours when we are the least able to disguise our real selves. In those hours, when we are so weak and fretful, the physician learns something more

[1] St. Luke iv. 38, 40; v. 12; iv. 40, 41; vi. 17, 18; ix. 2; xxii. 50, 51.

than our diseases; he learns our *characters*. The most delicate psychological skill St. Luke certainly possessed. I might refer you to the perplexity of Herod about our Lord; to the exquisite penetrating satire in those touches preserved by this Evangelist—' He that shewed mercy on him,' because the lawyer would not pronounce the Samaritan's hated name, and ' The Pharisee prayed thus with himself,' when there was no prayer;— to the delineation of Zaccheus; to Pilate and Herod making friends together; to the disciples believing not for joy and wondering, and returning to Jerusalem with great joy[1] after their Lord had left them. I might refer to the way in which he binds his materials together by an idea, as in the incident about Mary and Martha, which immediately follows the Parable of the Good Samaritan, for the purpose of completing the picture of the Christian life; and in the passage at the close of the ninth Chapter, where we have three different natures dealt with by Jesus[2].

---

[1] St. Luke ix. 7, 8, 9; xix. 1, 8; xxiii. 12; xxiv. 41, 52; x. 37; xviii. 11.   [2] Ibid. x. 38, 42; ix. 49, 62.

He loves too to tell what women did for Jesus. I need only mention the names of Elizabeth, of the Virgin Mother, of the woman which was a sinner, of Mary Magdalene and others which ministered unto Him of their substance, of Martha and Mary, of the weeping daughters of Jerusalem.

Perhaps it may be said, without irreverence, that this psychological skill finds its highest application in writing of the sacred Humanity of our Lord. From St. Luke's Gospel we learn much that is truest and deepest in relation to the Man, Christ Jesus. There is traced the successive development of 'the Holy Thing born of Mary,' 'the fruit of her womb,' into the Babe, the Child, the Man[1]. There are the statements, which sometimes seem incomprehensible, and sometimes degrading, as applied to one like Him, but which always 'requite studious regard with opportune delight.' For instance. 'When the time was come that He should be received up[2],'

---

[1] St. Luke i. 35, 42; ii. 16, 43.

[2] τὰς ἡμέρας τῆς ἀναλήψεως. ('As the time drew on to

—What can this mean, standing where it does, and speaking of the time before His death? Faith reads the riddle. '*Evangelistæ stylus imitatur sensum Jesu.*' Again. 'His sweat was, as it were, great drops of blood falling to the ground[1].' The Academic Shimeis of England, and France, and Germany, may seek for stones to fling at Him, from the dust of the garden. The French man of letters may cross Kedron, and wave out his scented blasphemies, leaving the unwholesome taint of Parisian patchouli under the Olives of Gethsemane. Why that Agony, those big drops, that burst of sorrow in which He was withdrawn[2] from His own? Why was He less firm than the martyrs, than Socrates, than the Stoics, than the Indian brave? A man who does not understand love and purity, sacrifice and self-denial, the fearfulness of sin, the holiness of God, the blessedness of communion with the Father to the sinless Man, and therefore the fearfulness of its suspension,

its accomplishment, in which He was to be raised by death into His heavenly glory,' Riggenbach), St. Luke ix. 51.

[1] St. Luke xxii. 44.   [2] ἀπεσπάσθη, Ibid. ver. 41.

cannot understand Gethsemane as represented by St. Luke.

2. There is a second characteristic of St. Luke's Gospel. It is not so much a logical conception, or historical framework, as an atmosphere in which it lies. It is the overpowering conviction that Christ is 'fairer than the children of men;' that the Gospel is full of joy and beauty, as well as of truth and power; so that its motto might be, 'Blessed are the eyes that see the things which ye see.'

(*a*) A well-known tradition makes St. Luke a painter. This tradition is not very ancient. It is not to be found in any writer before the sixth century. It is the thirteenth eentury before he appears as the patron saint of painters. He was not a painter. One of the most learned of living Roman Catholics writes, '*Negant id Heterodoxi omnes, ex Catholicis quoque haud pauci* ¹.'

The oldest tradition in Justin Martyr would seem to have believed that the Son of Man had literally no form or comeliness. There are two

¹ Dank, 'Hist. Revelat.' Div. ii. 285.

types of the image of the Son of Man in Christendom. In one, He is hard and stern, wan and worn; in the other, He has a soft fair beauty, with chesnut hair. 'I know not who he may be that will refuse to believe that He was beautiful[1],' says one who is a great master of convenient assumption. I do not know. Every Christian heart, indeed, may be sure that there was about Him moral beauty; the beauty of thought and expression, which 'radiates through the veil' of flesh and sense, which is consistent with sorrow, with a body destitute of the lines of grace, with the trials that make a man old before his time[2]. Half the ugliness of human faces is moral ugliness. There are, no doubt, faces beautiful in youth, which, as Plato says, we can easily foretell will be hideous in old age[3]. But infinitely worse are the sinister look of craft, the leer, the scowl, the heaviness, that are the visible expressions of petty designs puckering a network of lines, of unworthy thoughts, and ignoble lives. Half the

---

[1] Archbishop Manning.   [2] Appendix, Note 4.
[3] 'De Rep.' I.

beauty in the world is moral beauty too, which shines through the eyes that are pure and candid, and breathes through the lips that speak of truth and gentleness. Whatever His form and features may have been, He must have looked beautiful who said, 'And He layeth it on His shoulders.' Weary as He was and wan, white with exhaustion and dropped with blood, He must have looked beautiful who said, 'Father, forgive them.'

So the Evangelist who never painted the form of the Son of Man on canvas, or laid it in rich enamel, has given us the most attractive picture of Him[1]. In St. Matthew, He is Israel's Monarch; in St. Mark, He is the Son of God; in St. John, He is the Everlasting Word made Flesh; in St. Luke (while the title of the Lord, the Lord Jesus, is most frequently found[2]) we are almost tempted to think the emblem of the Man

---

[1] 'Esto enim eum fuisse peritum medicum, esto egregium pictorem, omnium præstantissimum est Evangelistam egisse.' Dank, 'Hist. Rev.' Div. ii.

[2] St. Luke vii. 13; x. 1; xi. 39; xii. 42; xiii. 52; xxii. 61; xxiv. 3.

more appropriate than that of the Ox, which yet suits so well the priestly story at the beginning, and the overpowering conviction of the Sacrifice at the end. For in St. Luke, He is pre-eminently the Son of Man; loving, pitying, pardoning a fallen race; anointed to preach the Gospel to the poor[1]; leaving the ninety and nine that He may bear the lost with all the strength and tenderness of that Divine Manhood; dying, and rising again, that repentance and remission may be preached to all. St. Luke may not have the lion strength of St. Mark, nor the eagle flight of St. John. The words of Christ recorded by him may be conversations rather than discourses. But the Christ in St. Luke is especially the Son of Man, fairer than the children of men;—the Child, wrapped in swaddling clothes and cradled upon a human breast; growing with true human growth in the Holy Home; the Man really tempted; not merely δακρύων as by the grave of Lazarus, but κλαίων with sobs of lamenta-

[1] ἔχρισέν με ('m'a messianisée,' Salvador), St. Luke iv. 18.

tion over Jerusalem[1]; the kneeler in Gethsemane, supported by His creature, yet so divinely drawn, that faith adores the Lord of Angels, strengthened by an angel, and the Son of God writhing like a trodden worm. Men complain of sameness in sacred art. Even the rationalist can teach us, that they 'who would give it freshness must steep their minds in the New Testament[2].' They must have present to them not merely the traditional Judge on the one hand, not merely the soft and nerveless beauty of a Syrian Adonis on the other; but the Son of Man, sublime in noble wrath as well as noble tenderness, who uttered the Parable of the Rich Man and Lazarus, as well as that of the Lost Sheep and the Prodigal. Not written by a painter, this is yet a painter's Gospel. From it come the favourite subjects :—the Virgin and Child, Simeon, the Scene with the Doctors in the Temple, the Ascension. A well-known politician has spoken of the ephemeral nature of the results effected by his craft in contrast with the im-

[1] St. Luke xix. 41.   [2] M. Réville.

mortal productions of Art, in the language of a humiliation so unfeigned that it would be improper to dispute its truth. 'Our labours seem to terminate with the day on which they are done, and to leave no trace behind them. It is the happy lot of artists to produce and bequeath to mankind that which becomes part and parcel of their permanent inheritance.' The picture in St. Luke's Gospel is a thing of beauty, which is a joy for ever.

(*b*) As St. Luke's is the Gospel of painting, so is it the Gospel of poetry. The parts of the Gospel which the imagination claims as most poetical are, in a considerable proportion, peculiar to it. The incidents of the Birth, the manger at Bethlehem, the Christmas song of the Angels, the arrival of the Shepherds, the swan-like song of Simeon at the Purification; all that 'idyllic serenity,' that softness as of a spring morning, contrasting so touchingly with the tears, and blood, and darkness of the close [1]; the home of Mary and Martha; the sinful woman with long hair;

[1] M. Réville, 'La Question des Evangiles.'

the words of tender beauty over Jerusalem; the meeting with the weeping women on the way to the cross; the walk to Emmaus; the Ascending Lord with uplifted hands.

All through St. Luke's Gospel, too, the ear can detect rhythmic bursts and choral vibrations. Listen to the refrain in the sixteenth Chapter, 'Rejoice with me, for I have found my sheep which was lost.' 'Rejoice with me, for I have found the piece which I had lost.' 'Let us eat and be merry, for this my son was dead and is alive again . . . . It was meet that we should make merry and be glad; for this thy brother was dead and is alive again.' Listen to the fuller and richer music of the processional of the Mount of Olives, 'Blessed be the King that cometh in the name of the Lord; peace in heaven and glory in the highest.' Listen to the Lord's words to the daughters of Jerusalem, so gloriously interpreted by Mendelssohn. Listen to that anthem-like close, which seems to come to us with the exultant yet measured voices of some noble cathedral, 'And they returned to Jerusalem, and were continually in the temple, praising and blessing God. Amen[1].' But more remarkably again is this the case in the opening chapters. You will remember the Song of the Angels, and those three others, so familiar to every son of our Church as the *Magnificat*, *Nunc Dimittis*, and *Benedictus*.

Alas! We may not enjoy this without question, as our fathers did. 'The evangelical history,' says M. Réville, ' is like a sun glittering in mist, light enough to make the disc look clear and radiant, thick enough for the rays of the circumference to be lost in a more and more undecided penumbra. The beginning and the end are lost to historical curiosity, and show themselves only to the mystic feelings of the religious man.' The Canticles are especially appealed to by Strauss and Renan as apocryphal, and indicative that the narrative is unhistorical.

Let us glance at them for a moment, and see whether we cannot find evidence in their con-

---

[1] St. Luke xv. 6, 9, 23, 24, 32; xix. 38; xxiii. 27; xxiv. 52, 53. See also ii. 20; vii. 50.

tents that they belong to the time to which they are assigned, and no other. The fact that they were *improvised* need produce no difficulty, for they were not composed according to strict rules of prosody, but in measured parallels: and such strains would come naturally to a pious Israelite.

Take the Hymn of Zacharias. What should we expect from him? The hope of Jesus Christ and of salvation, rising indeed a little beyond the Psalms, but still in Jewish colours, and under Jewish images. Precisely such is its character. The God whom Zacharias blesses is Israel's God. The mighty salvation is in David's house. It is the fulfilment of Prophecy in pursuance of the promise to Abraham[1]. The whole groundwork of the Hymn is Jewish. The time is felt to be a dawn at best, 'the day-spring from on high[2];' but there are vistas which let us behold the broad light upon the great deep.

Similarly with the Songs of the Blessed Virgin and of Simeon. Our Church uses them as daily Psalms, and applies them to Christ. But those

[1] St. Luke i. 68, 69, 73.   [2] Ibid. ver. 78.

who had seen the Incarnate Lord, who had beheld Him risen and ascending, would have spoken far more strongly. Their songs would have been more like 'Rock of Ages,' or 'When I survey the wondrous Cross.' They would not have been echoes of the harp of David so much as of the harps of heaven, 'Thou wast slain and hast redeemed us to God *by Thy Blood.*' 'This Hymn, if inconceivable earlier than Zacharias, is more inconceivable later,' says Dr. Mill. Such sunlit mountain-tops in the distance with such mists over the paths that lead to them, such a firm grasp upon salvation and redemption, such a clear view of its character as consisting ' in the remission of sins[1],' yet such silence as to its details, can only belong to the thin border-line of a period, which was neither quite Jewish, nor quite Christian. A little less, and these songs would be purely Jewish; a little more, and they would be purely Christian[2].

[1] St. Luke i. 77, γνῶσιν σωτηρίας ἐν ἀφέσει ἁμαρτιῶν.
[2] This argument is derived from Dr. Mill, 'Pantheistic Theories of the Gospel,' whose words I find that I have sometimes retained.

When we contrast the close with the beginning of St. Luke,—the narrative of the Ascension with that of Christmas in the second Chapter, we may find an inner evidence of its truth. What have we at Christmas? The Son of God condescends to an unspeakable humiliation; yet the Angel of the Lord speaks to the shepherds, and the air quivers with unearthly music. What have we at Ascension-tide? The victory is won. The shadows of Gethsemane and the clouds of Calvary have melted away. The hands of the High Priest are lifted up, and joy drops down from them like dew. And He is in the eternal calm, Who is deathless for evermore. Surely there are songs now. It may have been, as some of old thought, that God literally 'went up with a merry noise, and the Lord with the voice of the trump[1].' But if so, it was in heaven behind the veil, behind

---

[1] 'Ut Chrysost. notat, quod ad corporalem strepitum attinet, ascendit in silentio, fortasse non sunt visi neque auditi chori angelorum, ut in Nativitate; sed tamen dubitari non potest quin adessent angelorum legiones ineffabili jubilo deducentes Dominum gloriæ in gloriam suam. Psalm xlvii. 5.'—Bellarm. in Psalm. 335.

'the silence of the infinite spaces.' No echoes reach the earth. If man had invented, all the songs would have been for Ascension, all the silence at Christmas. Because it is Divine, the silence is at Ascension, and the song at Christmas.

What I desire you to remember is, that St. Luke is the psychologist among the Evangelists; that in his Gospels we find the elements of art and poetry in especial richness. Each Gospel brings out some aspects of Christianity with peculiar power; St. Matthew, its living connection with the sacred past of prophecy; St. Mark, the eternal power of the simple facts of the Redeemer's Life; St. John, its theology and sacramental depth; St. Luke, its beauty, its artistic and liturgical aspects.

IV. And now, if I were to draw my practical lesson from the text alone, I might say that it affirms the Life of our blessed Lord to be the sure basis of catechetical instruction. For the Gospel is not a system of *notions*, but a series of *facts,* and it is this which makes it universal and everlasting.

But as the subject which I have attempted to handle has been that of the fundamental conceptions of St. Luke's Gospel, so the main lesson which I would leave with you is derived from the delineation of our Lord in those wonderful pages. Schenkel, indeed, has ventured to say that, at the period when this Gospel was written, 'the direct impress of the unique personality of Jesus was fading dimly away into the background, and the exciting influence of the extraordinary and marvellous was needed, in order to lend attraction to the Life of the Redeemer.' And he proceeds to point out that 'the colouring of the miraculous is much stronger in the third Gospel,' alleging in proof what he terms 'the marvellous additions to the call of the first four disciples,' the raising of the widow's son at Nain, and the 'detailed accounts of the appearances of the Risen One in Jerusalem.' From such cold-blooded subtleties, I appeal to the facts of our consciousness.

Is there not in each one of us a sense of guilt and moral struggle? When the French king heard Massillon expound the seventh Chapter of the Epistle to the Romans, and speak of the two wills, the two men in the one man, he exclaimed, 'I know these two men.' So do all of us who have not risen to the height of our regeneration, whom 'the spirit of life in Christ Jesus hath not made free from the law of sin and death.' Life is a continued sense of discord; and the prospect of death makes us fear to walk forth as lonely spirits into a world untenanted of its God. But with this there is before us an ideal of holiness and beauty. Neither the hot fumes of dissipation, nor the vapours raised by sensual sin, nor the quick succession of paltry or unworthy pleasures, which seems to have taken the place of the rougher dissipation of other days in Oxford, can quite hide that from a young man's soul. Far over the head of him among you who to others and perhaps even to himself seems most lost, a bright peak towers above the clouds undimmed and undefiled; where, as he looks, he finds that a light lingers with magic beauty all day long, and a voice cries within his soul—There where the heaven is nearer; there where the feet have trodden of all whom you know, whose pure spirits have passed into the Presence of God; there, where you may bathe your burning forehead in the coolness of the eternal dawn; there is your home and rest.

The Saviour whom St. Luke describes answers to both. You will not, of course, understand me as speaking in the sense of the Marcionites of old who considered St. Paul the only Apostle, and St. Luke the only Evangelist. I speak of an aspect of the Saviour, present in all the Gospels, pre-eminent here, which makes one say with Bernard, '*Suavem magis quam sublimem et unctum non altum loquor;*' which makes it no exaggeration to pray with the Church, that 'by the wholesome medicines of the doctrine delivered by St. Luke, all the diseases of our souls may be healed.'

Christ, in St. Luke, meets our misery and greatness, meets our guilt and aspirations, meets the abject things which perhaps we are, and the noble and glorious things which we would be. He meets our sin by the word of forgiveness, by the Parable of Love, by the Anguish in Gethsemane, by Paradise offered to the dying penitent, by the Redeeming Death to lay hold on which is life. He satisfies, too, our yearnings after perfect holiness. St. Luke might, and indeed did, write better Greek than the other authors of the books of the New Testament. Perhaps we have heard a little too much of this since Jerome spoke of his '*sermo comptior, et secularem redolens eloquentiam.*' There has been too much tracing out of 'classical colour, if not of imitation,' in such expressions as θάμβος περιέσχεν αὐτόν[1], and others; too much desire to make out the sacred writer, 'acquainted with the principles of perfect composition, skilled in the use of them, and attentive to the effects which they must produce on the minds of his literate readers.' He did not belong to that republic of letters, the greater part of whose citizens, except a few children of genius, may be divided into the second-

[1] St. Luke v. 9.

rate men of letters, who succeed—to their own satisfaction—and the critics who, you know, 'are the writers who have failed.' Rather, we feel more intensely how great and Divine the Christ of the Gospel is, when the image, which from a mere literary point of view is imperfect, grows so radiant to every soul that contemplates it. We are led to say—O Son of Man! weeping over Jerusalem, kneeling under the olives, pardoning on the Cross, standing with uplifted hands to bless, we are sinful, Thou art holy. Thou art in the light and calm of the eternal peace; we are in the drift and spray, in the darkness and the deep. The shadows are closing round. Abide with us, for it is toward evening, and the day is far spent.

> 'Abide with us from morn till eve,
> For without Thee we cannot live;
> Abide with us when night is nigh,
> For without Thee we dare not die.'

SERMON IV.

ST. JOHN.

St. John i. 1, 14.

The Word was God. And the Word was made flesh.

I HAVE examined on previous occasions the fundamental ideas, the leading conceptions, of the Synoptical Evangelists. I shall attempt this morning and afternoon to deal, from a similar point of view, with the Gospel according to St. John.

I. The opening sentence of each of the Synoptics corresponds to the 'stand point' from which he surveys the earthly Life of the Redeemer. St. Matthew begins with a genealogy which marks out Jesus Christ as the child of promise and Prophecy, the son of Abraham, and heir of David. The whole of St. Mark's Gospel is an expansion of the title in the first verse, 'Son of God.' St. Luke at once professes that he writes with historical accuracy, and, when necessary, preserving the order of events.

The idea of the Prologue of St. John's Gospel is the Divine Glory of Christ in the Incarnation.

A great life, a life whose words and works influence mankind profoundly, is not sufficiently told by merely relating its facts and dates. What an enigma, for instance, is the life of Napoleon! How many of his biographies are mere masks concealing those bronze features[1]! We cannot understand any great and complicated life, good or evil, by merely recording the isolated events along which it moved. It is an organic whole, and must be reconstructed as such. That it is so with the life of Christ is confessed alike by Christians and by infidels. 'In histories of this kind,' says Renan, 'the great sign that we possess the truth is to succeed in combining the incidents, so as to constitute a logical and probable whole. What we have to recover is not the

[1] See Lanfrey, Life of Napoleon.

material circumstance which has passed beyond our control; it is the very soul of the history. A great life cannot be rendered by a simple agglomeration of facts. A profound sentiment of its subject must embrace all, and bind it into unity.' And the great Christian philosopher of the Middle Ages reminds us that a true Christology is the first and primary condition of a true Theology[1].

This, then, is the great leading idea of St. John's Gospel. *Given* the facts of Christ's Life, how shall we bind them into unity, and read them as a whole? What theory of His Person and Nature will give us a logical and consistent view? We may not believe that the alleged facts are historical; but if we do so believe, how can we reconcile them? For, in this very Gospel we meet with contradictory facts. On the one hand, the peasant guest called to the marriage feast; on the other, the Divine giver of wine. On the one hand, the weariness by the wayside well on the

[1] 'Circa quod, primum considerandum occurrit *de ipso Salvatore.*'

hot September day; on the other, the sublime self-consciousness of Him who said, 'If any man thirst, let him come unto Me, and drink.' On the one hand, the thorny crown, and the Form that elicited from Pilate the words of pity rather than admiration, 'Behold! the Man;' on the other, the majesty of the Body, which cannot be marred, which has between it and harm the great deep of type and promise. 'A bone of Him shall not be broken[1].' Such are some of the antitheses of the great Life, so nobly summed up by Keble:—

>   'Lo! He comes,
> Hungry, thirsty, homeless, cold,—
> Hungry, by whom saints are fed
> With the eternal living bread;
> Thirsty, from whose pierced side
> Living waters spring and glide;
> Cold and bare He comes, who never
>   Can put off His robe of light,
> Homeless, who must dwell for ever
>   In the Father's Bosom bright.'

In the Prologue to St. John's Gospel we have an answer to the questions suggested, a principle

---

[1] St. John xix. 36. Cf. Exod. xii. 46, Ps. xxxiv. 20.

by which we may harmonize the facts of that Life. St. John gives us a key which proves itself by fitting into all the wards of the lock. What Christ *did* and *said* becomes explicable only by knowing what Christ *is*.

Of the title, the Word, I will only say that it unites two lines of thought, one scriptural, the other metaphysical. In Genesis, in the Psalms, in Proverbs and Isaiah, the Word or Wisdom of God seems, with increasing clearness, to be made personal, and connected with the Divine Angel. But, further, the inspired thinker looks into the depths of his own mind, into the phenomena of *thought* and *language*. In the first he finds a faint type of the ontological relation between the Father and Son; in the second an illustration of the Incarnation[1]. By this great metaphysical conception (admired by Maine de Biran as sincerely as by Augustine), scripture is illustrated in its depths. The Logos of Philo, abstract and impersonal, a mere Platonic ideal according to

[1] See Döllinger, 'First Age of the Church,' i. 235, sqq.; Bull, 'Def. Fid.'

which God works, can only confuse us in dwelling on the Logos of John, who is a Personal Self-existent Being. The Son is the Word, because He has His Being from the Father. As a word is the formed utterance of the speaker's thought, He is the Word that the Father has outspoken into separate Personal Existence from the fulness of His Being.

Some who have not lost all reverence for Christianity speak as if St. John's Prologue added a difficulty for faith; as if St. Matthew or St. Luke on the Incarnation were comparatively easy to receive. Is it so, for those who think? Place side by side these statements. On the one side, 'when as His mother, Mary, was espoused to Joseph, before they came together, she was found with child of the Holy Ghost.' On the other side those four oracular propositions, 'In the beginning was the Word, and the Word was with God, and the Word was God. And the Word was made Flesh.' Which is easier to receive? There have been profound intellects who have confessed that the statement in St. Matthew almost repelled them. But every fact has its factual and its ideal aspect[1]. In St. John the fact of the Incarnation is lifted up, and flooded with the light of a Divine idea. If, in the Unity of the Divine Existence, there be a Trinity of Persons; if the Second Person of that Trinity is to assume the reality of flesh, and the likeness of sinful flesh; we can, in some measure, see why He needed the Tabernacle of a Body, framed and moulded by the Eternal Spirit to be His fitting habitation. The mystery of a Virgin Mother is the correlative of the mystery of the Word made flesh.

II. If we pass from this architectonic and presiding conception—to which St. John owes his title of *Theologus*, and his emblem of the eagle— we may conveniently trace the leading ideas of the spiritual Gospel under four heads, the Miracles, the Discourses, the Sacraments, and the delineations of Character recorded in it.

1. What is the leading idea in the Miracles of St. John's Gospel?

[1] Dr. Whewell, 'Inductive Philosophy.'

The Synoptical Gospels are full of miracles. The air is thick with them. It may be said that they are chiefly regarded as manifestations of Christ's power or evidences of His mission.

Now St. John, in his Gospel, certainly lays much stress upon the argument from miracles. Nowhere else is there a more frequent appeal to their weight as evidences. It is the Saviour's repeated assertion, 'The works that I do bear witness of Me, that the Father hath sent Me.' Yet in no Gospel are so few special miracles recorded. The turning of the water into wine; the healing of the nobleman's son, and of the impotent man at Bethesda; the feeding of the five thousand, and the walking upon the waters; the hiding Himself, not as a timid man crouching behind the pillars of the Temple, but as God hides Himself in nature; the restoration to sight of the blind man; the resurrection of Lazarus; the going back and falling to the ground of the band who came to arrest Jesus; and the miraculous draught of fishes after the Resurrection, exhaust the list[1]. How are we to account for this?

There can be no rational doubt, that he presupposes an acquaintance with them from other quarters, and so far bears witness to the earlier Evangelists. But there is another reason.

One miracle of each class is recorded, except that of which we read so much in St. Mark, the dispossession of demoniacs. Not that this last was foreign to his circle of ideas. He includes it in that triumphant sentence of his Epistle, 'For this purpose the Son of God was manifested, that He might destroy the works of the devil[2].' Indeed, it may be said without exaggeration that the notion of moral possession is peculiarly Joannic. 'One of you is a devil. Ye are of your father, the devil. The devil having now put into the heart of Judas to betray Him. After the sop Satan entered into him[3].' But the one miracle of each class recorded by him is a type,

---

[1] St. John ii. 1, 11; iv. 46, 54; v. 5 sqq.; vi. 5, 21; viii. 59; ix. 1, 41; xi. 1, 44; xviii. 6; xxi. 1, 11.
[2] 1 St. John iii. 8. [3] St. John vi. 70; viii. 44; xiii. 2, 27.

a sacramental action, an 'acted parable,' a golden ray streaming out from His presence and opening up a line of light far into the kingdom of God. Some are so interpreted by the Saviour Himself. For instance, the feeding of the five thousand leads to 'I am the Bread of Life.' The restoration of sight to the blind man teaches that He can couch the diseased eye of the soul, and let in the light upon 'the unlit gulf of ourselves [1].' In others, men, the least inclined to mysticism, have discovered a meaning of the kind. Thus Coplestone and Whately [2] agree with Augustine in seeing more than meets the eye in the wine of Cana. It is a type and image of all the work of Jesus. In the Bible the Law passing by His word, into something grander, richer, stronger. In our lives the world giving its best wine first; first romance and excitement, then the pleasure palling upon the jaded palate, and the wine of life upon the bitter and poisonous lees. But Christ reserves for His own grace upon grace, until, when the banquet is over, and

[1] St. John ix. 39.   [2] See Appendix, Note 5.

the Sacramental wine touches the lips for the last time, they can say to the Bridegroom of the Church, 'Thou hast kept the good wine until now.' Few Christians, indeed, would have much sympathy with the German Professor of Theology[1], who when Augustine finds in the raising of Lazarus the type of a sinner, long dead in sin, quickened to the life of righteousness, accuses him of 'trifling, ingenious perhaps, and pretty enough, but equally unworthy of the dignity of criticism, and the sanctity of Scripture.'

On the whole, it may be said that the miracles in the Synoptics *teach* as well as *prove*, and that those in St. John *prove* as well as *teach*. But the main idea of the miracles in the Three is to *prove*, while the main idea of the miracles specially recorded by St. John is to *teach*. To these especially are the words of Augustine applicable—'What our Lord did corporeally, He would have understood spiritually. For He did not merely work miracles for the miracle's sake, but that the things which He wrought might be *true* to those

[1] Clausen, 'Augustinus S. Scripturæ Interpres.'

who could understand them, as well as *marvellous* to those who beheld them. Our Lord worked miracles, to signify somewhat by those miracles, and that we should learn something more from them than simply that they were great, wonderful, and Divine[1].'

The Miracles in St. John, then, are viewed sacramentally and ideally.

2. The Discourses of Jesus preserved in St. John.

I need not remind you that the Synoptical Gospels are full of Parables. 'It is above all, in Parables,' says Renan, 'that the Master excelled. Nothing in Judaism had given Him the model of these exquisite pieces. He created it.' An eloquent historian of the Church writes[2], 'Born in the ranks of the people, leading the public life so common under an eastern sky, He addressed the multitude. When He was seen far-off on the border of the Lake, the masses gathered to hear from Him words at once sweet and strong,

[1] Tractatus in Ioan., ad init.
[2] M. Albert de Broglie.

majestic and familiar, alternately piercing the soul with barbs of fire, and charming the imagination by the touching grace of His Parables.' So characteristic of Him was this teaching, that St. Matthew *applies* to it the language of Asaph in the seventy-eighth Psalm: 'Without a parable spake He not unto them, that it might be fulfilled which was spoken by the prophet, saying, I will open My mouth in parables; I will utter things which have been kept secret from the foundation of the world[1].'

With this characteristic of our Lord's teaching in the Synoptics before us, it is, perhaps, somewhat startling for a simple Christian to be reminded—as he sometimes is, in no subdued tone —that in St. John no complete and regular Parable is preserved. Indeed, only two pieces with much external resemblance to Parables are to be found in the fourth Gospel—the comparison of the Good Shepherd in the tenth Chapter, and that of the Vine in the fifteenth Chapter. Nay, the very word does not occur, for the term translated

[1] St. Matthew xiii. 34, 35; Ps. lxxviii. 2.

Parable in our version is παροιμία in the original. Does truth, then, compel us to say to the reflective student,—You must make your choice sharply. If you are a Christian you must sacrifice a beautiful delusion to Him who will not be served by a lie. If your Lord spoke as Matthew reports, He did not, and could not, have spoken as John reports. You must surrender either Him who said, 'I will give you rest,' or Him who said, 'I am the Resurrection and the Life'—either the Jesus of the Synoptics, or the Jesus of John? A little consideration removes the difficulty.

(*a*) The *circumstances* under which the discourses of Jesus in this Gospel were delivered are different from those in which the discourses in the Synoptics occur. Every prudent teacher adapts himself to the taste and capacity of his audience. Indeed, the danger is that this complaisance should be carried too far. But there is an adaptation not unbeseeming the wise and good. The gentle strain of teaching which breathes of flowers and birds, the mountain and the lake, is not suitable to bigoted Theologians and atrabilious devotees living on the arid and stony soil of Jerusalem. Prelates and Professors of Divinity in the last generation, for aught I know in this, have been charged by those who call themselves 'sheep in search of pasture,' with preaching sermons possibly not fit for any place, but, if fit for any, only for University pulpits. There may be some truth in the accusation; though to men in 'quest of a good sermon,' the figs in the Church's basket are apparently always ' very naughty.' The great Bishop and Shepherd of souls reasons with Nicodemus, or with the Pharisees, in a strain very different from that which He adopts to the Galileans.

(*b*) Again; we find in this Gospel more words addressed to His own. Parables were not so fitting for continued instruction, addressed to those who were to go forth from His Presence to teach the world. Read the chapters from the fourteenth to the seventeenth. Those Divine deeps with human emotion quivering on them like light upon the surface of the sea, that soliloquy of the High Priest, pleading with His

Father, are absolutely peculiar to this Gospel, absolutely *unique*. Is it strange that the language which expresses them should be *unique* also?

(*c*) But, finally, if we have not Parables in St. John, have we not evidence in the words of Jesus there, of the tone of thought, which, under fitting circumstances, would create Parables? What are the comparisons of the Shepherd and the Vine but Parables in germ? Note how outward things are handled by the Master; with what associations He invests the water of the well, the bread with which He feeds the people, the light that falls upon the Temple at dawn, the grain of wheat, the vine, the sheep. From what manner of mind should we expect Parables? Surely from that to which nature is transparent, which in the noble words written by Southey for the monument of Butler, finds 'in outward and visible things the type and evidence of those within the veil.' If, then, in St. John's Gospel we find no Parables expanded, we find a number of Parables compressed.

This seems to be a natural place for noticing

one objection which has been confidently made against the historical truth of the Gospel. The objection to which I refer is based upon the undeniable likeness between the language of our Lord in the Gospel, and that of St. John in his Epistles. Are we to admit that we are forced to trace 'the monotonous tone' of John's own style in the Discourses, which can, therefore, lay no claim to historical accuracy? I will give the reasons which enable us to answer this question in the negative.

(*a*) The likeness between the style of the Discourses and that of St. John is somewhat overstated.

The word Logos, which we meet in the Prologue of the Gospel, in the first Epistle, and in the Apocalypse[1], is not applied by Jesus to Himself in any passage of His Discourses. Hengstenberg argues, and apparently with reason, that *light* and *darkness* are used with different intentions in the Epistle and Gospel; signifying in the Gospel the region of salvation, and the awful

[1] Apoc. xix. 13.

tract beyond, in the Epistle moral good and evil. The doctrine of propitiation and purification by the Blood of Christ is stated with less reserve in the Epistle than in our Lord's teaching in the Gospel[1].

There are other differences for an attentive student, which belong to deeper characteristics of thought and style. He who has made an attempt really to master the Epistle of St. John, will have been struck by two peculiarities. (1) As we read, we find a collection of apparently isolated divine γνῶμαι, of sentences generally short, and almost lapidary, in their strong simple incisiveness. These sentences superficially seem to be quite disconnected. Yet a connection there is, spiritual rather than logical, ethical more than intellectual, real not verbal. (2) A second characteristic is that, in passage after passage, the eagle of God seems to wheel round and round favourite thoughts. But it will be found that there is a perpetual line of advance, not mere spiral revolution. There is parallelism; but not

[1] Cf. 1 St. John i. 7 with Gospel iii. 16.

the 'mere monotonous parallelism, the cycloidal composition and eternal tautology,' with which the expression of Hebrew thought has been charged by Herder. It is a parallelism, or *oppositio cum accessione*, as critics have expressed it[1]. To take one instance out of many. 'He that hateth his brother is in darkness even until now.' Then, 'He that hateth his brother is in darkness.' Now note the accession to the parallelism, giving a solemn eloquence to the close of the verse, 'He is in darkness,' his inward condition. 'And walketh in darkness,' his outward life. 'And knoweth not whither he goeth,' to what unsuspected guilt, to what unsurmised punishment. Something worse still — worse than darkness, around, above, within. 'The darkness hath blinded him once for all,' he has lost the very faculty of light[2].

I will venture to assert that neither of these peculiarities is anything like so marked in the Discourses of our Lord in the Gospel.

---

[1] See Reiche, 'Comment. Criticus,' Tom. iii. in loc.
[2] ἐτύφλωσε, 1 St. John ii. 9, 10, 11.

(*b*) The opening words of the first Epistle show us that St. John would have found an insuperable moral objection to placing Discourses in the mouth of Jesus. 'That which was from the beginning, which we have *heard.*' This at once recalls to us the words of Jesus, more especially His discourses in St. John's Gospel. The very place of this clause in the sentence, where *hearing* stands out above *sight* and *handling*, shows us the reverence with which he regarded the words of the eternal Word. It shows us that he would have shrunk from the profanity of turning his Gospel into a fiction or a drama, and inventing language for the Incarnate Wisdom of God.

(*c*) But, if the similarity between the style of the Discourses and that of the Epistle is *exaggerated* by many, it is, at least, after all deductions, very *remarkable*. And, if we reject with indignation, on behalf of the Apostle, the supposition that he would invent language, and place it in the lips of his Master, can we find a satisfactory solution of the difficulty?

Assuredly we can.

Christ, in the days of His flesh, expressed His divine knowledge in words. In His teaching there were two elements, referred to by Himself in the antithesis, 'if I have told you of *earthly things* ... if I tell you of *heavenly things*[1].' 'Earthly and heavenly' is not equivalent to easy and difficult. But 'heavenly' comprises dogmatic objective truths, connected with the nature of God, and the counsels of His grace. 'Earthly,' again, assuredly does not mean earth-born or carnal. The word is not γήινα, but ἐπίγεια. To that Soul whose home was beyond the stars, in the bosom of God, things which seem to us the most heavenly, are on earth after all, ἐπίγεια. They are of heaven indeed, from heaven, even now '*in margine cæli*,' on the line which seems to blend with the heaven beyond. But they have for their subject-matter the teaching of truth, not as it is in itself, but as it meets with a creature like man, as it is capable of being morally tested and experienced by us. Others, then, recorded those

[1] St. John iii. 12.

words, which rather belonged to the circle of ἐπίγεια, or which made a greater impression at the time of their delivery. The Sermon on the Mount, spoken upon a height in Galilee to a great assemblage, sank into a thousand hearts, and found its way into the earliest memoirs. The conversation with Nicodemus by night, the dialogue with the Samaritan woman, the Discourse in the Temple, would not lie so near the surface of Christian recollection.

Of these two elements, then, in the teaching of Christ, there was one with which the mind of St. John had a constitutional affinity. He appropriated 'the heavenly things.' They sank into his soul. They were taken up into the substance of his intellectual and spiritual being. Those who have been much with the great masters of thought and language, though only through the medium of their books, show by their words and ideas the high company which they have been keeping. Tennyson, Browning, and Arnold impose the very faults of their diction upon a generation of poetasters. A very thoughtful theologian writes:—'I trace so distinctly to Bishop Butler the origin of the soundest and clearest views that I possess upon the human mind, that I could not write upon this, or any kindred subject, without a consciousness that I was directly or indirectly borrowing largely from him[1].' Common studies, and schools, and tutors, impress subtle similarities of literary form and colour. Modern Oxford men are liable to sudden conversions, and are drifted to havens upon the most distant shores of thought. But there is the old trick of voice. 'Cœlum non animum mutant.' The Autobiography of the Oxford politician is curiously like the Apologia of the Oxford Oratorian. But much more is this the case, where the charm of personal influence is added. 'I may be allowed,' says an eloquent writer, 'to take this opportunity of claiming, once for all, for the pupils of Arnold, the privilege and pleasure of using his words, and adopting his thoughts, without the necessity of specifying, in every instance,

---

[1] Bishop O'Brien, Preface to 'Two Sermons upon the Human Nature of our Lord.'

the source from which they have been derived¹.'
Those of us who, nearly twenty-five years ago,
on Sunday afternoons, used to listen with spellbound interest to the calm, sweet voice of the remarkable man who was then Vicar of St. Mary's, who told us of

> ' His misery's signs,
> And how the dying spark of hope was fed,
> And how the heart was soothed, and how the head,
> And all his hourly varied anodynes.'

will sometimes find a phrase, a word, a sentence coming to their lips or falling from their pen—or hear them in the sermons, and recognize them in the writings of others, which they can trace to a teacher, from whom they are now separated by the whole breadth of the spiritual world.

I have freely used analogies, drawn from our own days, and from living men, because I think they may enable us to feel more vividly how probable it is that the style of St. John

---

¹ Dean Stanley, Preface to 'Essays on the Apostolic Age.'

should be like that of the Discourses in the Gospel. Remember that that disciple was John, and that Master Jesus. Those favourite words, 'light and darkness, life and death, love and hate, truth and lie, world, abiding'—were not terms which he had taught himself to apply to the designation of his own ideas. He had heard them in the long golden hush of the summer-evenings by the shore of the Lake of Galilee; in the sorrow of the Guest-chamber; between the brook of Kedron and the Garden of the Agony; during the days when the Risen Lord spoke to them 'of the things pertaining to the Kingdom of God.' He had not only enshrined them in his memory. He had made them so livingly his own, had appropriated them so profoundly, that he could use them with unerring precision and definiteness. Expressions which occur in the Gospel historically and occasionally were taken into the Apostle's soul. No longer as it were in block, but rounded and smoothed like stones by the continual friction of the water, they appear in the Epistles, in a sententious, aphoristic form. 'Is it John, the son of Zebedee,' it has been asked, 'who could write these lessons of abstract metaphysics, to which neither the Synoptics nor the Talmud present any analogy?' Certainly, for he had heard them from Christ. In one instance, at least, he shows that he knew words previously recorded in the Synoptics. 'Jesus Himself testified that a prophet hath no honour in his own country[1].' Sometimes we can see that the thought latent in an expression in the Synoptics, is present to him. 'He spake of the Temple of His Body'— 'He dwelt among us[2],' is but the commentary upon the word in St. Matthew, 'There is something here greater than the Temple[3].' The Synoptical Jesus teaches nothing, we are told, but morality,—the Joannic nothing but Theology and metaphysics. What shall we say to such texts as these, 'All things are delivered unto Me of

---

[1] St. John iv. 44. Cf. St. Matthew xiii. 57, St. Mark vi. 4, St. Luke iv. 24.

[2] ἐσκήνωσεν, St. John i. 14; ii. 21.

[3] τοῦ ἱεροῦ μεῖζων ἐστὶν ὧδε, St. Matthew xii. 6.

My Father, and no man knoweth the Son but the Father, neither knoweth any man the Father save the Son, and he to whomsoever the Son will reveal Him.' 'If David call Him Lord, how is He his Son?' 'I thank Thee, O Father, Lord of heaven and earth[1].' Have not these sentences of Jesus in the Synoptics the same ring with the highest utterances in the spiritual Evangelist?

We may conclude without hesitation that John did not give language to Christ, but Christ to John.

3. We proceed to consider the leading idea of St. John's Gospel in the Sacraments.

In the earlier Evangelists their institution is recorded very fully. It is omitted in St. John. Why is this?

(*a*) It is true, and so far perfectly satisfactory, to answer that this Gospel was written considerably later than the others. The Church was fully organized. It enjoyed its weekly Celebration. It knew of the institution of the Eucharist, not

---

[1] St. Matthew xi. 27; xxii. 45; St. Luke x. 21.

only from the three Synoptics, but from the special revelation made to St. Paul[1].

(*b*) But the answer which it is the privilege of the Church's children to give, is deeper and more blessed than this, however valid it may be for apologetic purposes. St. John *does* treat of the Sacraments.

Can we doubt it? The sacred history and ritual observances of the Jews, even ecclesiastical institutions of the later date, are transfigured and glorified in this Gospel. Jacob's ladder, the Temple, the Serpent in the wilderness, the Manna, the Paschal Lamb, the beautiful ceremonial of drawing water in earthen pitchers from the fountain of Siloam at the Feast of Tabernacles in remembrance of the water gushing from the rock, —all these are spiritualized and idealized in St. John's Gospel[2].

And again, the holy Apostle's heart is so full of them, that in his Epistle he treats the

---

[1] 1 Corinth. xi. 23.
[2] St. John i. 51; ii. 21; iii. 14, 15; i. 29; vi. 32, 35; vii. 37, 40.

Sacraments with a mysticism, which is not dark to those who love.

'There are Three that bear witness, the Spirit, and the Water, and the Blood[1].' Of these Three the Gospel is full, section after section. He speaks of a Trinity of testimony on earth, the three 'genuine witnesses[2],' 'the shadow of the Blessed Trinity in heaven' of which he thought, but—so far as our evidence extends —did not *write*. And what is that testimony? 'The Water,' and the water of which the faithful know is that for the mystical washing away of sin. 'The Blood,' the Atonement, and the Cup by whose wine we are partakers of it. 'The Spirit,' the one Baptizer, the one Consecrator, for 'by one Spirit we are all baptized into one body, and have all been made to drink into one Spirit[3].' With these considerations before us, we shall not rob the Gospel of St. John of its sacramental jewels. The words of Jesus in the third of St.

---

[1] 1 St. John v. 7, 8.
[2] Professor Lightfoot 'On Revision,' p. 25.
[3] 1 Corinth. xii. 13.

John, addressed to an age full of baptismal ideas, can have but one meaning. No critical ingenuity, no 'licentious alchymony' of interpretation can ever prove that *water and the spirit* are equivalent to the *spirit without the water*. So with the sixth Chapter. There may be, and there are, objections to making our Lord's Discourse there *exclusively* sacramental. But to sever it from the Sacrament, to make it unsacramental, is contrary to common sense. It is impossible that the Apostles should not have been reminded of it, when the Holy Communion was instituted. It is impossible not to think of the Eucharist, as we read it now. It has been said by the most evangelical of commentators, 'that Jesus intentionally so framed His words, that while they treated at once and for ever of the spiritual fruition, yet that they fitted into the august mystery of the Sacrament when it was ordained, and which He evidently had in His mind[1].'

In this Gospel, then, St. John treats the Sacra-

[1] Bengel.

ments as he has treated so many other things. He spiritualises nature, history, ritual, miracles. But to spiritualise is not to evaporate, to 'subtilize into a metaphor.' He spiritualises Baptism and the Eucharist. That is to say, he shows us their ideal side; he lights them up from above and from within.

III. I defer the further consideration of the leading ideas of St. John's Gospel to my second discourse. Let me conclude with two thoughts of a practical kind:—

1. No thoughtful Christian can fail to have been struck by the fact that, except those few words which our Master 'with His finger wrote upon the ground,' He wrote nothing. He did not bow down over a table piled with manuscripts, and in hours of meditative thought during which He outwatched the stars, erect a monument which might be admired by a succession of sages and critics. He did not write out the complete text of an elaborate system of Theology. He went out into the throng of men. He spoke by the

highways and the lake-side, in words which, if they were high as heaven and deep as the transparent lake, were in form broad and popular. When we consider the analogy of the 'tables that were the work of God,' and 'the writing that was the writing of God[1],' and the value of books in excluding error and securing permanence — we ask why did He not write? There is one reason, derived from His nature. In great books the truest element of greatness is the conviction that we can trace the pathway of a superior mind in pursuit of truth. When he seems to have found it, the writer quivers with delight. With the Word made Flesh, truth cannot be an effort and a conquest—the conclusion toilfully drawn from premises laboriously acquired. Rather the Truth dwells in Him. He does not say,—After long communion with Divinely-inspired books, after long self-questioning, prompted sometimes by voices that seemed to come from the ancient hills, and the glory of the sunlit heaven, I gradually worked out My system.

[1] Exod. xxxii. 16. See Appendix, Note 6.

He does not say, I have *found* the truth. He does say, 'I *am* the Truth.' We may answer the question why Jesus did not write, with the philosopher of the Middle Ages. The thought of Jesus is preserved in a Diviner way, according to the great promise, 'I will put My law in their mind, and write it in their heart.' That which was done by the members was virtually done by the Head. It will be seen that, in this sense, the Gospels themselves may be looked upon as part of His teaching [1].

Let us, who are Christians, find here a stay for our souls in these unquiet days.

We are living with three creeds echoing round us, which are not our creeds. More boldly and with more developed meaning, since it was announced amid thunder and lightning, on July 18, 1870, the Ultramontane shrieks out the new dogma, which an educated man can scarcely accept otherwise than as a dogma of despair by the suicide of reason. Is it not practically this? 'I believe in a quasi-hypostatic union of the Holy

---

[1] See Appendix, Note 6.

Ghost with each successive Pontiff.' And, in daring contradiction to the Nicene Creed—whose structure classes together the creation of the Scriptures and the creation of the Catholic Church as the great external works of the Holy Ghost, Lord and Life-giver—Scripture and Church are cashiered to exalt one man above both. 'The appeal to antiquity'—ancient Church or ancient Word—'is a treason and a heresy.' Once more, there is the false creed of the Savoyard Vicar, feebly coloured with Christian language—I believe in natural religion without the supernatural; in a Christ better and purer than Socrates; in a Church of unlimited comprehension, without dogmas or miracle, or mysteries. As if natural religion was so natural after all; as if there could be a Christian religion without prayers and sacraments; as if every sacrament were not the commemoration of a miracle, and every prayer a sigh from the mystery of man's life to the deeper mystery of the life of God. There is a third creed, —I guard myself against saying that the theory of evolution is atheistic, or even necessarily inconsistent with the Catholic Faith—whose articles are these. I believe in law without a lawgiver. I believe in strength and visible reality working onward, first by spontaneous generation, afterwards by natural selection[1]. Something more. Still, as the Church with the light of an immortal hope falling upon her brow, which is turned eastward, where she looks (and will not always look in vain) for the flush of the promised dawn, chants, 'I look for the resurrection of the dead, and the life of the world to come,' outside there comes the response, half-sneer, half-sigh of the zoologist (misnamed anthropologist), 'I look for the fossilized bones of pithecoid man, and the everlasting death in a world, which is the only world that ever has been, or ever shall be.' Let us speak out, with full assurance of faith, the words of Jesus, 'I am the Resurrection and the Life,' 'The Father and I are one.'

2. A still more practical thought is suggested

[1] I refer to a Paper by a distinguished physician in the Proceedings of the Victoria Institute.

to us by the Miracles and Sacraments in St. John's Gospel.

(*a*) The mention of miracles before a University audience is apt to have a sound of battle. It suggests memories of metaphysical wrestling—matches in which Christian athletes, dead and living, and notably Oxford champions, have gained well-deserved honours. Let us not only maintain the *possibility* of the miraculous (the measure of whose probability is exactly that of the existence of God), and cling to the Gospel miracles as facts. Let us see in them Jesus turning the water of human life into wine, bringing food, and light, and love, and life, to the soul's hunger, and darkness, and loneliness, and death.

(*b*) So with the Holy Communion. There are those among us who are ready to act as its champions, to assert the reality of the gift which faith does not create but perceive. But let us all see to it that we not only believe about it, but use it, as the Gospel would teach us. There are young men fiercely tempted by the harlot-face of sensual sin, that looks so fair under the flickering lamplight of passion, so wan and haggard when God's daylight falls again upon the soul. There are some who have begun their Oxford life ill, in idleness and extravagance, which are a grievous wrong to their families and themselves. There are some who, without direct assault from unbelief, feel the faith within them dying in anguish in the intellectual atmosphere of the day, as men in the great forest fires, who, when the flames are miles away, perish by inhaling the burning air. There are some, it may be, in whom a new sense of sin and want is mysteriously awakening. Let them make the sixth Chapter of St. John their preparation for their next communion. Let them remember that these are the words of the Word made Flesh: 'I am the Bread of Life. He that cometh to Me shall never hunger, and he that believeth on Me shall never thirst.'

SERMON V.

ST. JOHN.

ST. JOHN i. 1, 14.

The Word was God. And the Word was made flesh.

WE endeavoured this morning to ascertain the leading ideas of the Gospel according to St. John. Its great leading idea is the Divine glory of Christ in the Incarnation. We saw, further, the points of view from which the Gospel would have us contemplate the Miracles, the Discourses, and the Sacraments. We proceed now to consider the leading idea in St. John's delineations of Character.

I. The profoundest thinkers, the most deeply reflective men, are not always the acutest observers, or the most judicious critics of individual character. Jesus alone both knew 'all men'—the delicate traits which distinguished one from the other, the individual souls who crossed the pathway of His life on earth—and also 'knew what was in man,' in our collective humanity. St. John, 'the Plato of the Twelve,' as he has been called, appears to have been endowed with some faint reflection of the power to read *men* as well as *man*. As we pierce through the mists of the past; as we try to give form and features to those whose ideal lineaments we have seen so often on the painter's canvas, or glorified by the sunshine in the Cathedral window; as we bring before us the Incarnate Lord, and the company by whom He was surrounded; we find that we owe yet more to St. John than even to St. Luke. The transparent simplicity of Nathanael; the noble humility of the Baptist; the sensual nature of the Samaritan woman; the rude bluntness of the blind man; the yearning of Philip; the passionate tenderness of Magdalene; the weakness of the sceptical Pilate; the contrasted characters of Judas Iscariot, of Peter and John, of the Judas who was not Iscariot; the melancholy of Thomas, doubting just because he loves: all these we owe, wholly or in part, to St. John. One cannot honestly sympathise with those who complain of the perpetual iteration and monotony of St. John. When a man accuses the Alps or the ocean of monotony, we may just suspect that there is a deficiency in himself. But while each is individually true, each also is a type of a class, with permanent and universal features. High above all is the figure of the Saviour, as St. John would have us see it. The power of that representation may be faintly illustrated by comparing one portion of St. John's narrative with the device whereby a painter has striven to represent it. We turn to the Discourse of the guest chamber. A great artist wishes to combine the Divine melancholy and Divine peace; the exquisitely blended joy and sorrow; the majestic sweetness of the 'Peace I leave with you,' with the reproachful sadness of 'Ye shall leave Me alone.' But he finds that he has no materials by which he can present to us simultaneously the deepening shadow of the human anguish, and the fulness of the sustaining love. And so just above the Lord reclining at the table a window is opened; and through it faintly and dimly are suggested rather than sketched Gethsemane, as it was an hour or two later, three sleeping forms and Another that kneels, and a winged shape flitting through the night towards the Olives, with a cup in his hand [1].

I shall, perhaps, best be able to bring out St. John's peculiar power of delineating character by directing your attention to his representation of the Baptist.

Before doing so I will just remind you by a brief quotation from Eusebius that St. John does, not indeed correct (as De Wette and Döllinger have said), but refer to the Synoptical books. 'After the fasting and temptation Matthew shows us the chronology of his book, saying, "Now when Jesus had heard that John was cast into prison, He departed into Galilee." [St. Mark and Luke in the parallel.] It is said that on account

---

[1] I speak here with a lively recollection of a beautiful article in the *Spectator*, which appeared, I think, in 1866, but which I have been unable to recover.

of these things, the Evangelist John, having been asked to relate in his Gospel the time passed over by the three former Evangelists in silence, and the things done in it by the Saviour (i.e. the things before the imprisonment of the Baptist), gave his assent. First by writing, "This beginning of miracles did Jesus;" then by mentioning the Baptist as even then "baptizing in Ænon near to Salim," and that he shows this distinctly by saying, "For John was not yet cast into prison[1]."'

What is the originality of the Baptist's character, even in the Synoptics? Not the ascetic garb and fare. Herein he did but profess to imitate Elijah. Not 'boldly rebuking vice.' Elijah and Micaiah stood up as bravely to Ahab. Not even 'patiently suffering for the truth's sake.' The mutilated body, 'stretched upon the threshold of Christianity,' only marks the *via dolorosa*, over which the whole army of martyrs have passed to their crown.

[1] Euseb. Pamph. Histor. Eccles. iii. 24. Cf. Tischend. Synopsis Evang. xxiv, xxvi.

It is to something else that we must look as constituting his originality.

The world recognises jealousy as the chief weakness of popular leaders and preachers. Such men are spiritual athletes, who cannot bear a rival. The greatest of popular preachers, the darling of Antioch and Constantinople, admits that he who can overcome this is almost like the disembodied spirits, whose lives, pure as the crystal stream, can never be darkened by any shadow of envy, or vainglory, or other sickly or unworthy passion. But the leader of a great party in a nation; the founder of a sect, which has vitality enough to live on for years; who was probably even regarded by some as Messiah, when St. John presided at Ephesus—that he should have bowed down in prostrate humiliation before a younger successor, this is original indeed.

The Baptist was distinguished by strength, independence, purity.

By *strength*. If ever there was a man unlike the lithe reed that gives itself to be tossed[1] by the

---
[1] σαλευόμενον, St. Matthew xi. 7.

wind, it was the Baptist. Your strong man is self-conscious. He has presided over the slow and painful elaboration of his character. He has looked on with satisfaction at the stiffening of his moral fibre into steel, and knows what it is worth. 'Humility,' it has truly enough been said, 'has never been a feature of strong Jewish natures.' Yet this strong man says, 'He that cometh after me is *stronger* than I[1].'

Independence is another of his characteristics. Yet, like David in God's presence declaring 'I will be base in my own sight,' so the Baptist exclaims, 'Whose shoes I am not worthy to stoop down and unloose.'

And above all the Baptist was *pure*. An effective moral teacher must 'In purity of manhood stand upright.' Never could he have brought men to repentance, if he had not himself repented. The words 'generation of vipers' would have been a mere scream of impotent rage, if he had not crushed the serpent in his own heart. Yet, in the presence of Jesus, that pure soul seems black

[1] $\textit{ἰσχυρότερος}$.

like the waters of a mountain-lake in the neighbourhood of the newly-fallen snow. The Baptism of water he knew; of the Baptism of fire, searching and sifting to the marrow, he recognized the need, 'I have need to be baptized of Thee.'

This abnegation it is which is so thoroughly original. Nothing in the Baptist's early life can account for it. Only sons, like the child of the aged Zacharias, are not commonly very unselfish. It ill becomes us, lounging in our easy chairs, the 'heirs of all the ages' in cookery and scientific comfort, to sneer at asceticism. But unnatural humility in one direction is sometimes made up for by unnatural pride in another. The haughtiest of the sons of men have worn haircloth next their skin, and lived upon fare less delicate than locusts and wild honey. The solution is not given by Renan, when he says, 'There is no other instance of the chief of a school receiving, with prostrate humility, the man who is to succeed and to eclipse him. But the Baptist was of the same age as Christ, and very young according to the ideas of the times—and youth is capable of any abnegation.' I know not what young men will think of the interesting quality here ascribed to youth. We who are older probably agree with Aristotle, who tells us in his Rhetoric, that 'the young are fond of honour, rather fond of victory. For youth desires superiority.' And that 'young men are μεγαλόψυχοι. For they have not yet been humbled by the discipline of life.'

I have dwelt upon this central characteristic of the Baptist at some length, because the way in which it is grasped by St. John illustrates one peculiarity of his Gospel. All his delineation of the Baptist brings out this note of his character with increasing clearness; 'He confessed and denied not, but confessed I am not the Christ.'— 'Behold the Lamb of God.' 'He must increase, but I must decrease[1].' It is the Baptist's picture seen in the light of his utter self-abnegation.

As in the case of this delineation of character, so is it with all others in this Gospel. The portraits of St. John are *idealized* pictures. But let

[1] St. John i. 19, 20, 39, 46; iii. 30.

us understand the word. We see the likeness of an ordinary face, endowed with a sort of vapid and unmeaning beauty; a coarse face, padded and coloured by a cunning hand. People recognise the likeness, and say, 'It is such an one, only a little *idealized.*' No! A face surprised with the glow of a virtuous feeling, or the visible inspiration of a triumphant thought; seen transfigured, interpreted in the light of an *idea,* of *the* idea of its life, this is an *idealized* picture. And such are the pictures in St. John.

We hear much of the 'unhistorical character of St. John's school.' But who are the really great masters of fiction? Not those who cover reams of paper with fine writing; but those who with the decided hand of genius strike off characters in a few bold lines,—those in whose pages the person and the words which he speaks are perfectly adapted. It has been said that in Shakespeare there is no image, however exquisite, which would not lose by being detached from its context, no speech which would not suffer by being placed in other lips. If it be so, either the old man, with the senile style of which we hear so much, was a mighty dramatic genius; or, there is truth in the words, 'That which we have seen and heard, declared we unto you[1].'

This may be the fitting place to bring before you a few of those minute touches in this Gospel, too minute and too delicate to have been deliberately invented; which, so far as they are not fancifully interpreted, do so much to establish the *verisimilitude* of a narrative. I mean, not by themselves to make it *probable* (the *probable* is that for the reality of which we can allege some reason) but *likely*, 'bearing the closest resemblance to that which is classed in our minds under the predicament of existence[2].'

I select a few instances.

(*a*) 'His disciples came, and marvelled that He talked with the woman: yet no man said, Why talkest Thou with her?' 'The disciples looked one on another, doubting of whom He

---

[1] 1 St. John i. 3.
[2] Blanco White, quoted in Bishop Hampden's 'Philosophical Evidences of Christianity.'

spake. Now, there was leaning on Jesus' bosom one of His disciples, whom Jesus loved. Simon Peter, therefore, beckoned to him, that he should ask who it should be of whom He spake [1].'

With us men, familiarity breeds contempt. No dignity will assert itself against a certain degree of intimacy. 'No man is a hero to his valet.' These passages, quite incidentally and informally, show that it was not so with the Word made Flesh. Those simple men were with Him in familiarities, that would have discoloured anything that was not heavenly, and belittled anything that was not Divine. They trod the same road; they rocked in the same boat; they rested in the same chamber; they partook of the same coarse fare; they drew out of the same scanty purse. Man exacts much of the idols in whose presence he lives; he sets them up easily, but pulverizes them upon very slight provocation. One bitter word, one fretful or peevish sentence, one self-seeking action, one questionable look, would have dethroned Him. But 'all our experi-

[1] St. John iv. 27, xiii. 22, 24.

ence is reversed.' With us, familiarity breeds contempt. But as the disciples grew more familiar with Him, He surrounds Himself with an awful dignity upon which they dare not intrude[1].

(*b*) 'I go not up to the Feast,' (for οὐκ, not οὔπω, is certainly the true teaching). A charge of falsehood, or of fickleness, obviously lies against these words. Yet they are fearlessly written down, though their meaning does not appear upon the surface.

One like the Word made Flesh must and will use words in His own sense. Our great Christian moral philosopher has said that 'a man may be under a moral obligation to say what he foresees will deceive, without his intending it.' At all events, Jesus will *weight* these words with the meaning of His own soul. He is on the journey of which we read towards the close of the ninth Chapter of St. Luke. To Him there is but one going up to Jerusalem, one Feast. 'My going up is not to this Feast[2].'

---

[1] See Bushnell, 'Character of Christ.'
[2] See Appendix, Note 7.

(c) 'Jesus wept.'

Just before 'He was troubled.' Rather *troubled Himself*[1], for a certain Divine decorum tempers all that we read of Him, and He is not represented to us as possessing a nature to be played upon by passive emotions. Why? We cannot fully tell. Perhaps, we may conceive the case of a physician coming into a room, where friends and children are sobbing over one whom they supposed to be doomed, himself weeping in sympathy, though sure that he can heal. But at least, this shows us that we have a real Christ. It was never invented. The imaginary Christ would have walked majestically up the slope of the Mount of Olives, and, standing with a halo of the sunset round His brow, have bidden the dead man rise. The real Christ was a dusty and wayworn man, who wept over the grave, and lifted up His eyes. The reality teaches us that the dead are not raised by a stoic philosopher, with an eye of ice and a heart of marble, but by One who is very Man, with the tender weakness that is more

---

[1] ἐτάραξεν ἑαυτόν, St. John xi. 34.

beautiful than all our strength. This is more majestic as well as more moving. But could St. John have invented it[1]?

II. There are two more leading ideas in St. John's Gospel.

1. It was intended to show the growth of belief and unbelief round our Lord's Person. We see the tide gathering, until at last it goes over the head of the victim. Three miracles form three points round which it gathers—the healing of the Bethesda, the cure of the blind man, and the resurrection of Lazarus.

Let us take another important instance.

We have seen that the special miracles recorded by the Synoptics are omitted by St. John, with the exception of the Feeding of the Five Thousand, and the incident which immediately follows it. Why do the circles intersect here?

No doubt the importance of the Discourse in the synagogue at Capernaum, and the symbolical character of the miracle, are sufficient to account

---

[1] See M. Godet, 'Sur l'Evangile de S. Jean.'

for this. Historically also these passages, taken in conjunction with the beginning of the seventh Chapter, show us, that while the Synoptics mainly follow the Galilean Ministry, and St. John that in Jerusalem,—yet that the fourth Evangelist was perfectly acquainted with the Galilean Ministry. For the Passover, mentioned in the sixth Chapter, occurred in April, the Feast of Tabernacles in the seventh Chapter, in the end of September, or the beginning of October[1]. St. John then tells us that in the interval, 'Jesus was *walking* in Galilee,' which perfectly describes one main external feature of the Galilean Ministry[2].

But, assuredly, one object which the Evangelist had in view was to trace out the progress of belief and unbelief. And in the fifth and sixth Chapters we have two forms of unbelief contrasted. The unbelief of Jerusalem, 'the Jews

---

[1] St. John vi. 4, vii. 2, 14.

[2] περιεπάτει ὁ Ἰησοῦς ἐν τῇ Γαλιλαίᾳ, St. John vii. 1.—' Ex Hebraismo, ut alia verba eundi, *versor, commoror.* vii. 1, xi. 54, in quibus locis simul respicitur quod Jesus *ambulando docebat*.'—Bretschneider, Lex. Man. s. v.

sought to kill Him,'—the unbelief of Galilee, 'This is an hard saying, who can hear it?' 'Many of His disciples went back, and walked no more with Him¹.' Types of two forms of unbelief in all ages! One is sad or contemptuous, another fanatical. One sneers, another strikes. One sighs, another grinds its teeth. One would kill Him if it could; another turns upon its heel. One curses Him, and loathes the sacred wounds; another would only pierce His loving heart by leaving Him alone.

The very miracle is mentioned here, because it led to unbelief.

2. The fourth Gospel is throughout pervaded by the idea of human witness, of human testimony to Christ, from the Baptist; from the disciples; from the Jews at Jerusalem, during the first Passover; from the people which were with Him when He called Lazarus out of the grave; from the Pharisees who believed, but did not confess; from Himself, who saw the blood and

---

¹ St. John v. 18; vi. 60, 66.

water coming from the pierced side; from Pilate and Caiaphas.

St. John delights to arrest and make permanent the burning cries of confession wrung from the hearts of man. From the Baptist, 'Behold the Lamb of God!' from Nathanael, 'Rabbi! Thou art the Son of God;' from the Samaritan woman, 'Is not this the Christ?' from Peter, 'We believe that Thou art that Christ, the Son of the living God;' from the people, 'When Christ cometh will He do more miracles than these which this man hath done?' from the officers, 'Never man spake like this man;' from the blind man, 'Lord, I believe;' from Martha, 'I believe that Thou art the Christ, the Son of God;' from Pilate, 'I find no fault in Him;' from Thomas, 'My Lord and my God.' Wonderful music! drawn from the heart of man by the hand of Faith, running up the scales from its faintest and lowest note, 'Thou art the King of Israel,' to its grandest and richest harmony, 'My Lord and my God.'

And here it may be mentioned, how with a grave and gracious irony St. John, again and again, takes up the supposed objections, which in reality were so many proofs. Thus: 'Then said the Jews among themselves, whither will He go, that we shall not find Him? Will He go unto the dispersed among the Gentiles, and teach the Gentiles?' Easily answered by Gentiles, who were addressed by the Apostle from a Gentile city, in a Gentile language[1]. Again. 'Some said, Shall Christ come out of Galilee? Hath not the Scripture said, That Christ cometh out of the seed of David, and out of the town of Bethlehem, where David was[2]?' And so, when men allow themselves to exclaim triumphantly, John knew nothing of the birth in Bethlehem—we can only say that they know little of John.

(*a*) One idea of this Gospel, then, is that it is a Gospel of witness, of human witness, to our Lord. Faith is a plant which is intended to rise upward by twining round the pillar of evidence. We may see how much plausibility there is in the sneering assertion that the 'Joannic school used, without scruple, the principle which was

[1] St. John vii. 35.   [2] Ibid. ver. 42.

destined to become Hegelian, it *ought* to be so, ergo, it *is;*' and 'that it is, more and more, an admitted principle of criticism, that if we would write *history*, we must mould our conception after the type in the Synoptics, not after that in the fourth Gospel.' We may point to such a passage as the opening of the fourth Chapter, ('When the Lord knew how the Pharisees had heard that Jesus made and baptized more disciples than John, He left Judæa and departed again into Galilee,') with its matter of fact but valuable historical explanation. Here, again, St. John refers to and illustrates the Synoptics. For the fact that John was cast into prison would not, by itself, have determined our Lord's departure from Judæa into Galilee, which indeed was part of the dominion of Herod Antipas. But every attentive reader may see for himself, that one leading idea of this Gospel is founded upon the great historical principle of the validity of *human testimony*—the great safeguard against scepticism and fanaticism. 'If we receive the testimony of men' to the effect that 'Jesus is the Son of

God,' writes St. John in his Epistle, with evident reference to his Gospel[1]. The very form of the expression[2] shows that we do assuredly receive such witness, not as Christians, but as rational men, according to principles which recommend themselves naturally to the unsophisticated human intellect.

(*b*) But again, as 'the witness of God is greater,' so this Gospel is full of *Divine witness* to Jesus. Hence the mention of the attesting voice from heaven, 'I have both glorified it and will glorify it again.' Hence the intense conviction that the Scriptures are 'they which testify of Him,' that 'had they believed Moses, they would have believed Him.' Hence the accumulated reference to Type and Prophecy in the narrative of the Atoning Death. In a mere human historian there might have seemed to be no more of deep purpose in the particular cruelties inflicted by the rude soldiery and the furious mob, than in the shape of the tangled knots of sea-weed flung by the spring-tide upon the beach. But every

---

[1] 1 St. John v. 9.   [2] εἰ λαμβάνομεν.

incident in the central event of the history of humanity is to his eye arranged 'by the determinate counsel and foreknowledge of God.' The lots upon the poor vestment, that wrapped the wasted form, were cast by a Divine Hand. The vessel with vinegar, the sponge and hyssop, were not there by chance. The perfection and dignity of that Body, which seemed so helpless, were guaranteed by the rubric of the Divine ritual in regard to the paschal lamb, 'Not a bone of him shall be broken.' The thrust of the soldier's lance is in the dark background of Zechariah's prophecy, and written upon the very Body that shall come in the clouds of heaven. 'They shall look on Him whom they pierced.' The Evangelist's spirit sails over the deep of Scripture as over an Equatorial Ocean, but on the far horizon of prophecy he sees its Southern Cross.

(*c*) His own Miracles are yet another witness in this Gospel of witness. 'I have greater witness than that of John ; for the *works* which the Father hath given Me to finish, the same works that

I do, bear witness of Me, that the Father hath sent Me[1].'

Miracles are called by four names in the New Testament. Of these three are thrown together in several verses[2]. Miracles are δυνάμεις, as manifestations of Divine Power; τέρατα, (or θαυμάσια in one passage) as producing holy awe and amazement; σημεῖα, as moral evidences to all who are right disposed.

The fourth synonym for Miracles is *Works*, frequently used by St. John.

St. Paul's use of *works* throws instructive light upon this. By works, he never means *good works*. They are opposed to πίστις, as an inward principle of heavenly life to the sum total of the product of the weakened and enslaved powers of the natural man[3]. Works are those things which it is *natural* for man to do, being what he is.

---

[1] St. John v. 36.

[2] Acts ii. 22; Hebrews ii. 4. See the works of *Antichrist*, 2 Thess. ii. 9.

[3] Tholuck on Romans.

Even so with Christ's works. They are, as the Baptist in St. Matthew's Gospel heard of them[1], such works as Christ would do, such as were natural for Him to work. There are many speculative difficulties about miracles. We are used to reasoning from miracles up to Christ; may we not reason from Christ down to the miracles? Given a being like Christ, the Word made flesh—the Christmas Eve, the Star of the Epiphany, the glory of the Transfiguration, the riven rock, the rent vail, the opened grave, the Ascension to the heaven of heavens, are but the fitting framework of that divine picture. Voices from the silence which men deem eternal, and rays from the world which to them is darkness, may well haunt with their echoes, and lighten with their glory, the pathway of a Life like that. The sick healed, the demoniacs dispossessed, the bread multiplied, the winds hushed, the waves on which He trod as securely as if they were Galilean meadows upon a summer's day, all these cease to be unnatural

---

[1] τὰ ἔργα τοῦ Χριστοῦ, St. Matthew xi. 2.

—'His Name is wonderful.' Therefore the supernatural is His natural element; supernatural works are natural for Him to do. For the believer, the Person of Christ witnesses to His miracles. For the unbeliever, the miracles witness to His Person.

(*d*) There is a fourth testimony in the Gospel of testimony—the witness of Jesus to *Himself*—to His glory, to His sinlessness, 'Though I bear record of Myself, yet My record is true [1].'

Consider what this witness is. If any of us know a holy man, we know a humble man. The holiest men are the most conscious of their own sinfulness. It is not a fashion of speech. It is not cant or hypocrisy. The writer, who is perfectly satisfied with his own lines, is not a poet. The painters or sculptors who have no noble dissatisfaction with their work, may be ingenious and dexterous, but they are not artists. They have none of that straining forward to an unattained and unattainable ideal of beauty, which is the heritage of genius. So too the man who is per-

[1] St. John viii. 14.

fectly content with his own spiritual condition may have a mechanical regularity of habit. He may be a respectable Pharisee. But he is utterly without that *saintliness* which is, as it were, the genius of goodness.

Now Jesus had the loftiest idea of duty. He was also the meekest and humblest of men. Yet in His Life there is one fundamental difference from the lives of the saints. They are full of burning words of penitence: they are burdened with cries of confession. But we have long Discourses of Jesus. We have one soliloquy with His Father in the seventeenth Chapter. Yet there is no confession of sin. He can bare His noble breast to His enemies, and say, 'Which of you convinceth Me of sin?' He can go further; He can declare, 'The Prince of this world cometh, and hath nothing in Me.' Further yet—in those solemn moments when death is near; when moral natures, seemingly made of the strongest granite, crack and crumble before the fire of eternity; He can lift up His calm and trustful eyes to Heaven, and say, 'I have glorified Thee on the earth, I have finished the work which Thou gavest Me to do.' And with this we know that His spiritual insight was so keen and piercing, that not one mote could have floated upon the tide of His purity without being detected by that eagle eye,—that one speck or stain could not have rested on the very skirts of the garment of His humanity, without soiling in His sight the raiment that was as white as snow. This holy Man, with the highest idea of duty; this humble Man, who prays falling upon His face; this keen-sighted Man, who sees further into sin than any other, declares that His life and the perfect rule of goodness are in unbroken harmony. What witness is comparable to this witness of Jesus to Himself?

On the whole, then, the leading ideas of St. John's Gospel are these. First, it is, in a special sense, the Gospel of the Incarnate Lord. Then it is the Gospel in which the Miracles and Discourses of Jesus, the Sacraments of the Church, and the Characters of those who are delineated, are spiritualized, and viewed from a certain high and ideal stand-point. Finally, it is the Gospel which exhibits the growth of belief and unbelief; the Gospel of witness—the witness of men, the witness of the Father, the witness of Scripture, the witness of miracles, the witness of Himself.

III. In bringing this series of sermons to a close, I will but add one parting word of exhortation to my younger brethren.

There are many voices claiming the allegiance of your intellect. Judge all teaching, and all masters, in the last result, by the words of Christ. And for this reason.

'The Word was God, and the Word was made Flesh.' He had not only a true Human Body, but a 'reasonable Soul,' a true Human Intellect. In the one Person of Christ, there are two forms of Wisdom, two manners of knowledge. The finite intelligence and the Infinite, the human and the Divine, differ as the created from the Uncreated, as the relative light of the Incarnate Word from the absolute light of the Uncreated Word. But they are at one, and work to one end. Of these two lights, the lesser is not darkened, but increased by the greater. Our knowledge of ourselves rests upon the ultimate fact of *consciousness*; but He knew Himself, not only in the light of consciousness, but in the light of God. 'I am not alone, but I and the Father that sent Me[1].' Therefore the Human Mind of Jesus is never alone[2]. And the processes and development of the Human Reason rest upon the Infinite Wisdom.

If this be the true idea of Christ, what shall we say of His word? Must there not be perpetual power, consummate beauty and originality, perfect truth, in the words of the Word made Flesh?

We may smile bitterly with Schenkel at the simple men, who looked upon the very number of the four Gospels as divinely harmonising with the quarters of the world, and the principal winds, and the form of the cherubim. We may be

---

[1] St. John xvi. 32. See Appendix, Note 8.
[2] St. John v. 30, viii. 16–18, xiv. 10. See Gratry, 'Les Sophistes,' 335.

amused, if we will, at Augustine's quaint yet beautiful conceit, in expounding and applying to St. John the text in the Psalms, 'The mountains shall bring peace, and the little hills righteousness to the people.' The old man, with the shadows and the sunlights of the hills of Africa present to his mind, says, 'The mountains are great souls, like that of John; the little hills are ordinary ones, like ours. Never should we have received the light of faith, unless those great mountain-tops, lighted up by the heavenly wisdom, had passed them on to us.' Yet as we read the words of Christ, and think who spoke them, we need not be ashamed to cry with Bernard, 'I hear not Moses now. To me he is of stammering lips. Isaiah's lips are unclean. Jeremiah cannot speak; he is a child. All the prophets are mute. *Ipse, ipse, quem loquuntur, ipse loquetur.*' Well may we, in our own church, stand when the Gospel is read, out of reverence to the Master's word, and burst forth into the chant of glory. Therefore let us be of good courage. One may tell us that the photograph, which has been projected on the plate of the Gospel by light from Heaven, is yellowing, and will have faded away in another generation. Others may tell us of the prejudice of our Christian training. These dogmatic prepossessions are, no doubt, respectable for the children of clergymen, whose education was possibly conducted by country Parsons. But all the products of the human intellect are subjected to necessary laws. A day will come, and soon, when another Brucker or Cousin will teach all educated men to treat dogmas—even the dogma of the Word—with the same cold and disinterested impartiality, wherewith they might study the Fauna and Flora of the Silurian epoch. Others again may inveigh against the narrowing effect of dogma, and the repression of the moral and spiritual by it. But the picture cannot fade, if it is drawn on an eternal plate, by eternal light, and renewed again and again. The system may pass away if it be a mere product of the human mind; not, if St. John be true, when he speaks of the *message* which we have heard from him, and *announce* (mark the authoritative, the half-sacerdotal word, ἀναγγέλλομεν) *announce* unto you[1]. Dogma may be repressive. But is the eagle of God chained to earth by dogma? This leading idea of his Gospel, this dogma of the Incarnate Word, is the ambient air upon which he floats. The view which he shows us is like one in a southern land, where the prospect is not bounded by any milky film or mist in the lustrous air, but by the weakness of the organ. The *dogmatic* evangelist is the *spiritual* evangelist also. Cling then to these words. As you would keep the hope of immortality and the belief in God; as you would be pure amid the fires of youth, and hopeful in the terrible monotony of middle age; as you would have pardon for your sins through the redeeming Blood, and strength for your weakness in a life-sustaining Sacrament; as you would have everlasting Arms to uphold your human mutability, and a pierced Hand to wipe away your tears;—cling to them. They cannot fail you. They are the words of the Word made flesh. Enter this porch with prayer, and like Moses of old

---

[1] 1 St. John i. 5.

'you shall hear the voice of One speaking unto you from off the mercy-seat, and He shall speak unto you[1].' And as at the Lesser Entrance in the Greek ritual—the entrance of the Gospel, considered as enshrining Christ, who is the Wisdom[2]—there are hymns amid the darkening shadows of the sunset-hour to the 'Holy and Joyful Light;' so in the spiritual darkness that is settling down upon the world, you shall be able hopefully to pray, that you and all 'the Church being enlightened by the doctrine of the blessed Apostle and Evangelist St. John, may so walk in the light of his truth that it may at length attain to the light of everlasting life, through Jesus Christ our Lord.'

---

[1] Numbers vii. 89.

[2] So 'the 24th Psalm is recited in the Synagogue, at the carrying back of the volume of the Law, the *written Word of God*, into its shrine: we see here the return of Christ Himself—the *Living Word*—into His Heavenly Shrine.'—Bishop Wordsworth, ' Holy Bible,' Psalms, p. 34.

APPENDIX.

NOTE 1, p. 6.

'THE most ancient interpretation of this passage is that which St. Jerome heard from some learned Jews, who became Christians. It refers it to that passage in the 11th of Isaiah, where we read of a Branch growing out of the roots of Jesse. But the Hebrew word is *Nézer*. St. Matthew's meaning in that case would be—He who contemptuously gives to the Son of David the name of Nazarene accomplishes Prophecy, for this Nazarene is the true *Nézer*, the Branch of God, growing out of the root of Jesse.

'I think that there is another and more striking explanation. In Hebrew the name Nazarene is pronounced *Nozri*. The Jews at this day call Jesus by this name in contempt. But the same word *Nozri* signifies also "my Saviour," "my Protector." This expression is not, indeed, found in any isolated Messianic passage in the Old Testament, but all the Prophets, without exception, represent Him as the Saviour and Protector of Israel. St. Matthew means to say—It is a stumbling-block to you that the Son of David has been brought up in this poor Nazareth. In your wish to insult Him by this reproach, you do but accomplish Prophecy. When you call Him *Nozri* you announce His truth: you fulfil that which the Prophets foretold: you declare that He is your Saviour and Protector. This is one reason why He was to come from Nazareth, that those who insult Him under the name of *Nozri* should be obliged to glorify Him by saying "My Redeemer and Protector," which is, in point of fact, conformable to the word of the Prophets.'—Riggenbach, 'Life of Jesus' (French translation), pp. 203, 204.

Note 2, p. 7.

Καὶ ἄλλως δὲ ἐπλήρωσε τὸν νόμον, τούτεστιν ἀνεπλήρωσεν· ὅσα γὰρ ἐκεῖνος ἐσκιαγράφησε, ταῦτα οὗτος τελείως ἐζωγράφησεν· ἐκεῖνος τὸ μὴ φονώσῃς, οὗτος τὸ μηδὲ θυμωθῇς εἰκῆ. ὥσπερ καὶ ὁ ζωγράφος οὐ καταλύει τὴν σκιαγραφίαν ἀλλὰ μᾶλλον ἀναπληροῖ.—Theophyl. in Matt. v. Tom. i. 25. See a long Catena of passages from the Fathers to the same effect in Hammond's interesting note, 'Practical Catechism,' Lib. ii. Sect. 3, pp. 110-114.

NOTE 3, p. 57.

'The Latin copy of St. Mark's Gospel at Venice is proved not to be an original by irrefragable arguments. (*a*) From the errors of the copyist, (*b*) the various corrections, (*c*) the markings of the sections, (*d*) the style of the Latin. (*e*) This MS. has the preface by St. Jerome *written in the same hand*. (*f*) The character of the writing, and the orthography, are perfectly distinct from those of the Apostolic age. From all this it appears that this MS. is to be reckoned among the oldest Latin copies, if not of the fifth, at least of the sixth century; but that it cannot be an autograph of St. Mark the Evangelist.'—Dank, 'Hist. Revelat.' Div. ii. 282, 283. This Latin MS., known to critics as 'for' (i. e. Foroiuliensis) is assigned by Tischendorf to the sixth century.—'Nov. Test.' Præf. ccxlix.

NOTE 4, p. 98.

'M. Renan supposes that Jesus had one of those exquisite faces which sometimes appear in the Jewish race ('Vie de Jésus,' p. 80). It is remarkable that the East, in its mosaics and pictures, has always presented a Christ with a severe face, while the West has sunk to a soft, fair face, with a high colour. I must confess that the grand

mosaics of the Calvary at Jerusalem, and of the beautiful Byzantine apses, possessed by Greece and Italy, go more directly to the soul. The gentle Galilean cannot properly be represented with light hair, nor with a curled beard, gracefully divided. Art should avoid the hardness of the mosaists without falling into the insipidity of our painters.'
—Michon, 'Vie de Jésus,' i. 197, 198.

Note 5, p. 124.

Bishop Copleston's Sermon on the Marriage in Cana was published, along with several others, by Archbishop Whately in 1854, in a volume called 'Remains of the late Edward Copleston, D.D., &c.' (J. W. Parker, West Strand, London). It is the Eleventh Sermon in the collection. The Archbishop's note to it is :—

'There is something remarkable in the history of this Sermon. The main substance of it had been stated to me by a friend who had been struck with a sermon he had heard in which this view was taken. I repeated this to Dr. Copleston, who was so much struck with it that he thereupon composed the following discourse, which I heard him preach for the first time. From recollection of this, I afterwards myself wrote a sermon, which has since been published.'

The Bishop of Killaloe, who has been good enough to

furnish me with the information contained in this note, believes that the original of these sermons is one by Saurin.

Note 6, p. 146.

Jesus wrote no book.—See Neander, 'Life of Christ,' p. 104. The whole question is admirably discussed by Thomas Aquinas.

' *Summary.*

' It might seem that Christ ought to have written: for—

' 1. Writing is best for an immortal doctrine. St. Luke xxi. 33.

' 2. Analogy of Old Law. Deut. xxiv. 1, xxxii. 16, xxxi. 18, xxiv. 12.

' 3. Exclusion of error. "Some are wont to be surprised because the Lord Himself wrote nothing, so that we must believe others writing of Him. This is specially said by that class of Pagans, and of others, who will not openly blaspheme, and who allow Him surpassing wisdom, but simply as Man. They say that the disciples gave Him more than His due, so as to call Him God."

' Yet it is matter of fact that He wrote nothing.

' *Answer.*

' 1. The more excellent mode suited the most excellent

teacher. Cf. St. Matt. vii. 1. The Analogy of Pythagoras and of Socrates, who wrote nothing.

' 2. Most excellent doctrine cannot be cramped into books. Cf. St. John xxi. 25. St. Augustine says, 'Not that there would not be local room, but *capacitate legentium comprehendi non posse.*'

' 3. Due order through disciples to people. Mystical reference to Proverbs ix. 3.

' Again,

' 1. What was done by members was done by the Head. *Qui facit per alium facit per se.*

' 2. Old law might be written, but 2 Cor. iii. 3.

' 3. Those who believed not Apostles would not have believed Christ.'

Cajetan adds some good thoughts, showing how this was more worthy of Christ's divine glory.

'Christ teaches, *like God*, not by writing. Analogy of God's mode of teaching natural things.

' Jeremiah xxxi. 33. He will prove His doctrine one of spirit and life, not of death and the letter. Christ, knowing that this internal teaching was reserved to Him as Lord, committed not His writing to paper, as if the doctrine must perish if the writing were lost, which He would preserve for ever by an inward light.'—D. Thomae, 'Summa Theologiæ cum Commentariis Caietani.' Quæst. XLII. Art. IV. Tom. iv. p. 142.

NOTE 7, p. 164.

The germ of this explanation is found at an early date. Ἔλεγεν ὅτι οὐκ ἀναβαίνω, κ.τ.λ. οὐ γὰρ ἐψεύδετο, μὴ γένοιτο —μυστηρίως γὰρ καὶ πνευματικῶς διαλεγομένου τοῖς αὐτοῦ ἀδελφοῖς οὐκ ᾔδεισαν τί ἔλεγεν· ἔλεγε γὰρ αὐτοῖς μὴ ἀναβαίνω εἰς τὸ ἱερόν ἐν τῇ ἑορτῇ ἐκείνῃ μηδὲ εἰς τὸν σταυρὸν τοῦ τελειῶσαι τέως τὴν οἰκονομίαν τοῦ πάθους αὐτοῦ.—Epiphan. (quoted by Tischend. 'Nov. Test.' p. 594); cf. 'Christo vero ille fuit dies festus, quo passione suâ redemit mundum,' August. de Q. Nov. et Vet. Test. Qu. 78.

NOTE 8, p. 180.

Aquinas discusses the question whether our Lord had other than Divine knowledge. His answer is, that the affirmative is involved in the verity of His Incarnation. 'Filius Dei naturam integram assumpsit, i.e. non solùm corpus sed etiam animum, non solùm *sensitivam*, sed etiam *rationalem*. Nihil naturalium Christo defuit, quia totam Humanam Naturam assumpsit. Ideò, in sextâ Synodo damnata est positio negantium in Christo esse *duas scientias*, vel duas sapientias ... Minus lumen non offuscatur, per majus, sed magis augetur, sicut lumen acris per lumen solis. Et hoc modo lumen scientiæ non offuscatur sed clarescit in animo Christi per lumen scientiæ inditum.' (T. Aquinas, Part. III. Qu. IX. Art. I.)

www.ingramcontent.com/pod-product-compliance
Lightning Source LLC
Chambersburg PA
CBHW021733220426
43662CB00008B/823